. . . quaeque ipse . . . vidi, et quorum pars magna fui.
   Aeneid, Book II

UNDER QUAKER APPOINTMENT

The Life of
Jane P. Rushmore

By
Emily Cooper Johnson

Philadelphia
UNIVERSITY OF PENNSYLVANIA
1953

Copyright 1953

UNIVERSITY OF PENNSYLVANIA PRESS

Manufactured in the United States of America

Library of Congress Catalog Card Number: 53-10517

Published in Great Britain, India, and Pakistan

by

GEOFFREY CUMBERLEGE: *Oxford University Press*

London, Bombay, and Karachi

Foreword

The subtitle of this book might well have been, in old-fashioned language, *The Life and Times of Jane P. Rushmore,* for Emily Cooper Johnson has made amply clear the intimate connection between Jane Rushmore and that segment of society in which she lived.

Jane Rushmore was born a Hicksite Quaker at a time when Hicksite and Orthodox viewed one another with suspicion and distrust. She has dwelt within the area of the Philadelphia Yearly Meeting (Race Street). She has worked for the Hicksite branch of the Society. And she has lived to see the healing of the great schism within American Quakerism, having contributed herself to the reunion of the two branches. Jane Rushmore's history is in no small part the history of Hicksite Quakerism in the last eighty years.

The outstanding American Quaker in the first half of the present century was Rufus Jones. To bracket him with Jane Rushmore might seem to yoke together an unmatched team. Nevertheless, they have been the two most influential Friends in this country in recent memory, and they belong together. Their differences are obvious. Rufus Jones belonged to the Orthodox side of Quakerism. He was a scholar of international renown, known for his studies of mysticism and for his contribution to the history of Quakerism. He was a leader among Friends, widely known and sought outside the Society, the prime mover and guiding spirit for many years of the American Friends Service Committee. Jane Rushmore was little known outside the Society of Friends. She served as secretary and clerk rather than chairman of the major Quaker

FOREWORD

movements and organizations. Rufus Jones was a public figure; Jane Rushmore worked quietly behind the scenes.

And yet these two Quakers, warm friends for years, are strikingly similar in many respects. Both were primarily teachers. Both were interpreters of the spirit of Quakerism. Both wrote extensively. Both gave their lives to the Society of Friends. Both had great practical wisdom. Both spoke with homely wit and penetrating wisdom. When either spoke, the audience gave them a rapt attention accorded no other Friend of recent years. Both were moved by a vision of mankind which enabled them to transcend the divisiveness of the group into which they were born and to contribute mightily to the unification of the Society of Friends.

Emily Cooper Johnson has written the biography of a great human being, and in the process she has contributed another chapter to the history of Quakerism.

JOHN W. NASON

Acknowledgments

Although the preponderant body of material in this book comes from Jane Rushmore herself, additional information and certain critical estimates have been supplied by other persons. Cordial acknowledgment of this help is made to Edward W. Evans, Thomas A. and Eliza Ambler Foulke, Anna Stubbs Groff, Ellen Pyle Groff, Anna B. Hewitt, Edith W. Jackson, Arthur H. Jenkins, Edward C. Jenkins, Marie C. Jenkins, the late Howard Cooper Johnson, Alice L. Miller, James A. Norton, Sarah W. Passmore, Alexander C. Purdy, the late Robert Pyle, Howard G. Taylor, Charles N. Thompson, Emma B. Wallace, George A. Walton, and Clarence A. Wesp. For permission to quote from letters I am also grateful to the late Charles F. Jenkins, John W. Nason, Katharine H. Paton, J. Roland Pennock, and John H. Wood. In the preparation of Chapters V and VI the staff of Friends General Conference was most helpful. At all times the facilities of Friends Central Bureau were generously made available through the kindness of its entire staff.

In addition I am especially indebted for critical reading of all or parts of the manuscript to Hannah Clothier Hull, Marguerite Hallowell, J. Barnard Walton, Sarah F. Splint, J. Edgar and Edith Chambers Rhoads, and William Hubben; for help in publication to Richmond P. Miller and Henrietta S. Jaquette; and for great assistance in the preparation of the manuscript to Lois Comings Bertholf, Helen Griffith, and Miriam M. H. Thrall.

E. C. J.

Contents

		PAGE
FOREWORD by JOHN W. NASON		v
INTRODUCTION		xi

CHAPTER		
I	A QUAKER HOUSEHOLD IN THE SEVENTIES	1
II	SHARPENING THE TOOLS	15
III	"JANE, CHESTER COUNTY, PA."	31
IV	SOCIAL PLEASURES AND A SOCIAL CONSCIENCE	49
V	SEVEN YEARLY MEETINGS AT WORK TOGETHER	67
VI	BIENNIAL PILGRIMAGE	91
VII	AT THE HUB	107
VIII	AS A REASONABLE SERVICE	127
IX	FROM THE CLERK'S TABLE	149
X	UNDER WEIGHTY APPOINTMENT	159
XI	CRUMBLING WALLS	175
XII	THE ACTIVE EIGHTIES	193

Illustrations

	FACING PAGE
JANE P. RUSHMORE (about 1900)	44
RACE STREET MEETING HOUSE	110
JANE P. RUSHMORE, LITT.D., 1952	196

Introduction

The divided existence of the two Philadelphia Yearly Meetings of Friends will probably approximate a century and a quarter by the time the Separation of 1827 has ended and Race Street and Arch Street have become again one Yearly Meeting. Of the period during which American Quakerism has been divided into "Hicksite" and "Orthodox" branches, Jane P. Rushmore's life covers nearly three-quarters, and her active participation in the affairs of her Meeting more than half. It is the half, moreover, about which little is as yet written. Much has been analyzed and explained concerning the Separation; far less has been said of the enterprises which each group developed, and of the first gropings toward renewed intercourse which are now culminating in organic union.

Jane Rushmore was a very young woman when she came to teach in a rural Quaker neighborhood in Pennsylvania, a neighborhood typical of a large proportion of the Hicksite communities, and she spent the major part of her working life at the hub of Race Street Yearly Meeting's organized activity as secretary of Friends Central Bureau.

Her whole experience lay in the Hicksite fold. She learned its deep concerns, watched its development, often laid a guiding hand upon its growth. She saw that the Hicksite branch was no mere splintering to be either dried up and shucked off or ultimately grafted back on the main stem of Quakerism with the unfortunate divagation graciously overlooked. Rather the Hicksites were, certainly in their own estimation, throughout this era upholders of an essential part of the Society of Friends' original testimony, whose purity they carefully guarded. They believed that in accepting, as all Friends do, the continuing revelation of God to man, they must preserve the freedom of each individual to interpret the Scriptures and hold what seems true to him. Human beings, they felt, will not always translate the Voice of God into the same words. Liberty must be accorded to those whose perception of truth may differ from that of the majority. All honest search must be respected. It was this passion for liberty of interpretation which held them apart from the wave of the evangelical movement then spreading over the country. It was this that made them largely indifferent to doctrinal pronouncements and ultimately placed them in the group of "liberal" denominations.

The dignified jealousies, the cool ignorings, the careful withdrawals of an earlier generation from contacts with "the other branch" are only amusing now, and a caution to us who may be tempted into similar faults. But they, too, were a part of the Quaker life Jane Rushmore experienced and understood.

She has, however, more than remembered in wide extent and with remarkable accuracy a long flight of Hicksite years. She sees that they were a significant and expanding era. Important movements occurred inducing new life and a widened conception of usefulness for this group of Friends. The emerging ideas and undertakings made their mark upon all those who watched them with eager interest or participated in them in even minor ways. Their influence was especially appreciable on Jane Rushmore, herself a power in many of them, merely an onlooker in a few, but always aware of and appraising their growth. Among them were the establishment of George School, the rise of the Buck Hill Falls Quaker settlement, the evolution of Friends General Conference, the increase

INTRODUCTION

in the number and effectiveness of working committees in the Philadelphia Yearly Meeting, the widening reach of the *Friends Intelligencer,* and, especially, the development of new understanding among all branches of Friends through the agencies of the American Friends Service Committee, the American Friends Fellowship Council, the World Committee for Consultation, the Young Friends Movement, local united Meetings, joint Yearly Meeting committees in many of the major fields of work, and the establishment in Philadelphia of the General Meeting. Whether or not Jane Rushmore has been integral to these activities, she has observed them with a degree of detachment that has made her able to distinguish the structural from the incidental lines, to see the long direction of a sometimes wandering track.

She flatly refused, however, to undertake the writing of the narrative herself. The only solution seemed to be to introduce a sort of amanuensis to whom she was willing to talk. So each week for most of a long summer the scribe would present herself at the door of the little white house adjoining the meeting house lawn at Riverton, N. J. With Emma Wallace's warm smile, there also pressed the exuberant welcome of Vickie, barking through her long black hair. As Jane approached, a gray streak would shoot from behind her and slither, apparently without legs, up the stairs. Their cat does not like company.

In the south half of the living room Jane would settle into a corner chair from which she could look outdoors in two directions. As the summer opened, roses climbed in luxuriant bloom over trellises, iris and poppies flamed in the flower beds. Bird books are always within Jane's reach if a new visitor should join the familiars of the stone terrace. Her books of poetry are opposite to her;

INTRODUCTION

nearer at hand is the newest crossword puzzle thumbtacked to a breadboard. From the wall looking down upon her crowded desk are the Dutch great-grandmother, the grandfather of flavorsome personality, the greatly cherished Aunt Mary, and Deborah F. Stubbs, whose home was home to Jane for fourteen years.

Jane had to be persuaded to have any part whatever in this undertaking. It was against her judgment. In the end she agreed to help, saying: "I seem to be a kind of maypole around which the streamers of Philadelphia Yearly Meeting are to be wound, pretty much covering up the pole."

CHAPTER I

A Quaker Household in the Seventies

In the farming country thirty miles southwest of Albany, N. Y., John Underhill Rushmore and his wife, Sarah Drake Rushmore, were bringing up their family. Their white clapboard house stood by the road between Preston Hollow and Cooksburg in the southernmost corner of Albany County. Actually the family considered that they lived in Preston Hollow, although they were about halfway between the two villages, scarcely more than a mile apart. The fields rose steeply behind the modest L-shaped dwelling, and the Catskill Creek flowed beside it. To see the beautiful wall of the Catskill Mountains rising to the south one might either climb certain of the sharp hills on John Rushmore's ninety acres, or go to his father-in-law's, Israel Drake's, beyond the neighboring village of Potter Hollow, where a fine panorama opened directly from the front door.

The Rushmore house, cosily planted between the road, the creek, and a hill, scanned the neighbors as they passed on their way among the three tiny hamlets whose greatest distance of separation was less than four miles. The little group of villages was isolated in a sense that would be unknown anywhere in the United States now. Seven miles an hour was fast travel for a horse in hilly country, and twenty miles a day about the limit of his journey. With the nearest train at Cairo, twelve miles off, the usual means of transportation had to be the stagecoaches, whose drivers entertained their passengers with stories of more or less accuracy, largely to impress city arrivals. Telephones, radio, electrically driven domestic machinery were undreamed of. The mail came in by stage every other day to Cooksburg. For their newspaper the Rushmores read the *New York Semi-Weekly Times*.

It had not occurred to the children in the family to think of themselves as remote from the world or in any way lonely. To begin with, there were five of them. The middle child, Jane Palen, named for her grandmother, was the first girl. She had been born on January 28, 1864. Her older brothers were Charles and Edward, and after her came two sisters, Mary and Anna. All of them had plenty of ideas. They had to invent their own games and make their own playthings, a great stimulus to originality. It was a laborious job to construct a cart, but a wonderful satisfaction when it was finished. Remembering the excitement of spring floods in their creek, they reproduced its terrors by routing water from their little pails on to houses made of corncobs which were gloriously washed downstream. Like children today they liked trains, but their coaches were split pumpkins, running not on electricity but on boy power. Influenced by stories of the still recent Civil War, the children waged mighty battles in the sand lot where willow sticks could be recruited in as large armies as desired. Pebbles of different sizes were collected into ammunition dumps of shot, balls, and shells and hurled at the foe with the greatest abandon. When it was necessary to transport troops elsewhere the trains were ready for loading the soldiers, who stood straight and close in the soft fiber of the pumpkins.

Some bright schemes did not find favor with the parents. Shooting arrows from the upper door of the hayloft at carriages bearing Methodist neighbors to Sunday afternoon service, and then ducking out of sight of the baffled victims, was met with rebuke that made the children feel

A QUAKER HOUSEHOLD IN THE SEVENTIES

they had committed a very wicked act. They enthusiastically attended revival meetings in a nearby church until their elders discovered that their purpose was to learn how to mimic and ridicule in their own play at home the emotional scenes. But if these games were frowned on, there was plenty of imagination to invent new and better ones. And besides such lively entertainment as the children could always work up for themselves, various community events, in which the Rushmore family had full share, gave a little extra excitement. For instance, every fall after the harvest was in, a big farmers' picnic brought a great crowd together near Rensselaerville. A brass band, speeches, quantities of food, made the date a special event of first magnitude. The children loved it.

Jane took a good deal of responsibility in caring for the little girls, but she wanted to play with her brothers. They said they wouldn't have a 'fraid cat with them, so they made up a test of valor. Jane must run without flinching across the high beam above the partly filled hayloft. Though terribly frightened, she did it and won her accolade. The boys accepted her. Unconsciously they taught her more than physical prowess and agility. On one occasion they raced up a ladder leaning against the side of the house and climbed on the roof. Jane started to follow. Midway she saw the ground far below, was suddenly scared, and called for help. Her brother shouted to her, "Of course you'll fall if you look at your feet. Look up!" That admonition she remembered gratefully all her life.

The open hospitality of the Rushmore home was well known and brought visitors from far and near. They were usually Friends. There was still a great deal of itinerant religious service freely undertaken by those men and women who felt called on to make the journeys. It was spoken of as "traveling in the ministry." Small and scattered groups of Quakers were in large measure encouraged to uphold their faith by these devoted souls who had "felt a concern to travel in Gospel love" to more or less distant parts. The concern would have been laid before the home Meeting of the Friend who felt it; then, if approved, it was often supported by a superior Meeting and the person was released to do his or her best. The practice, of course, dates from the very beginnings of Quakerism and is followed occasionally to the present day. In the middle of the past century it was very common. When the welcome travelers came to Preston Hollow they always stayed at the Rushmore home.

The tiny meeting house was situated in Potter Hollow, between the Rushmores and the Drakes. Its official name was the Rensselaerville Monthly Meeting, and by the 1870's it had become very small. The few Friends still in the neighborhood expected it to die, and accordingly before the end of the century it did.

In its fold, however, during Jane's childhood was one strong figure, that of her grandfather, Israel Drake, a minister of vigor and ability. Buttressed with a minute from his Monthly Meeting, he undertook long journeys, sometimes for three months, with his horse and carriage, visiting Friends as far away as Pennsylvania and Virginia. Some of his stay-at-home neighbors considered that he neglected his farming to go to Meetings, but, his granddaughter remarks, he prospered better than his brother who did nothing but work. His wanderings, moreover, never caused him to neglect his community when he was at home. With no hospital in the area, Israel Drake took a man ill with smallpox and deserted by everyone else into his own barn and nursed him, happily without any spread of the disease to the family. As a good preacher and a liberal thinker, he was often called to attend funerals of those who were members of no church. Once when he was asked if he would speak at such an occasion he replied, "It must be understood that I am not engaged to preach, but I agree to attend,"* thus emphasizing his Quaker trust in the immediate leading of God for the need of the hour, be that need audible word or silent prayer.

Israel Drake had been an ardent abolitionist, and during the days of slave labor in the South would eat no cane sugar, but only maple. His farm had been a northern outpost of the Underground Railroad. Such fugitives as came by this rather unfrequented route were helped on the last lap of their journey to Canada. When the Civil War was over, he maintained his interest in the newly liberated men. Not many of them had arrived to settle in the vicinity in Jane's childhood. She remembers the first colored man she saw. She was about five years old when she was with her grandfather in Hudson and, meeting a dark-skinned passer-by, asked what was the matter with that man's face. There was no objection to the color in the mind of Israel's grandchild, it was merely a surprising fact to be accepted. In a somewhat later summer a Negro was employed to help with the harvesting on the Drake farm. The other hands would work in the fields with the newcomer, but refused to eat with him. Thereupon Israel Drake carried his own dinner to the outside kitchen and ate with the colored man, and Jane did the same. Her grandfather, greatly pleased, considered this

* This incident is also related in Irvin C. and Ruth V. Poley, *Friendly Anecdotes* (New York, 1950), p. 35.

a sign of grace. He was mistaken. Jane cultivated the friendship of this worker because he let her ride home on the hayload.

These grandparents, living only a couple of miles from the Rushmores, were always an intimate part of the life of the growing family. They were the only grandparents the children knew, as John Rushmore's father and mother had both died early. But the Drakes' was a familiar home where the strong personality of Israel made a deep impression on the youngsters.

His wife, Jane Palen Drake, had other ideas for her namesake than riding the hay wagon or romping with the boys. The elder Jane came of a rather more aristocratic strain than the Drakes. Her parents had sailed to America from Holland; she was well educated for her time, reserved, fine looking, holding her head a little high. Her family felt that she had married somewhat beneath her, and her husband was a bit deferential to her. She always accompanied him on his journeys, near or far. At home she was benevolent to her neighbors, but did not greatly mingle with them socially. She sought to train her granddaughter in the ladylike accomplishments she valued, especially fine needlework, at which she was expert. Samplers she considered too gay. She herself had embarked on a long undertaking of embroidering in silk floss on a silk base a map of the two hemispheres. This she felt had an educational purpose, especially as the place names were carefully entered. But she failed to interest little Jane, who regarded this as a regrettable use of geography and a waste of time. She did not succeed in making the child into a needlewoman.

The interest in education, however, ran in strong current straight down the generations. The senior Jane's daughter, Sarah Palen Drake, and her sister Mary had been sent a long distance from home to obtain better schooling than the immediate locality could provide. If Jane Drake was determined that Sarah and Mary should have a good education, Israel was equally insistent that they should go to a Friends' school and be among Friends. The suitable combination was found with John and Rachel Jackson, who conducted a private school for girls, the Sharon Female Seminary, near Darby, Pa. Perhaps Israel Drake had visited it in his travels. In any case, John Jackson was a well-known minister who traveled widely, a strong follower of Elias Hicks, and therefore known to the Drakes. The school which he and Rachel operated was one of the older ones for girls. There Sarah formed many associations with Friends in the general area of Philadelphia, the most intimate of which was with Hannah Griscom of Woodbury, N. J., who later married Charles Marot. After Sarah finished at the Jackson school (one was not "graduated" from a Friends' school in those days) it was therefore natural for her parents to approve of her accepting an appointment to teach at the Woodbury Friends School, boarding with the Griscom family. She returned to Potter Hollow to marry John Rushmore in 1859.

Like his father-in-law, John Rushmore was a man of strong personality and independent ideas. He was a Republican in a community of Democrats. In a day when use of the "plain language" was still a powerful tradition among Friends even if no longer an actual principle, John refused to use it, saying that it was not plain. By this he meant that terms like "Fourth-day" and "Eighth month" were not quickly understood. Nor did he see any value in wearing "plain" clothes, and never adopted them. He was very stiff in some ways, and his absolute probity was well established. A strong believer in local option and holder of the office of excise commissioner, he was open to no bargaining in the matter of enforcing the law. But when the tavern keeper's baby was sick and needed milk from an assuredly healthy cow, the man came to John. The sale completed, the man was about to leave when he remarked with some feeling, "Mr. Rushmore, I hate like sin to buy a cow from you. You've spoiled my business. But you're so honest that when my baby got sick I was afraid not to."

Yet John was far from being an austere man. He and Sarah made themselves an active part of the social life of the region. Not only traveling Quaker preachers found hospitality in the Rushmore home; frequently ministers of other churches who were attending district or county conventions, or for other reasons passing through, were entertained at dinner. John enjoyed himself greatly arguing good Hicksite doctrine with these gentlemen, challenging them on their own ground of theology. He was an ardent disciple of Elias Hicks, born when the fires of the Separation were still hot; in his mind the truth lay clearly with the great Long Island apologist.

Sarah Rushmore disliked theology and took no part in the dinner-table discussions, but she shared her husband's concern for the religious life of the neighborhood. They brought up their children to go to meeting every Sunday as a matter of normal procedure, without exceptions and without question. There were too few Friends' children to make special arrangements for them, so Sarah became, and for many years remained, the superintendent of a union Sunday School held in the Friends' meeting house, the only building in the community devoted to religious purposes. In spite of caring nothing for doctrine, she wielded a considerable religious influence. She was a nature lover, a good botanist, and she loved to grow flowers. She always had time to tell her children a story, or to do puzzles with them. Each child, of course, had specific tasks in the economy of a farm household, but if, while she washed dishes, Jane wanted to memorize poems her mother would help her choose them.

Her husband, cordial in his relations with other denominations, was inevitably asked to go on the list of those making donations to the Methodist minister's salary. A Quaker who had conscientious scruples against what an earlier generation regarded as a "hireling priesthood" could scarcely accede to such a request. Church suppers were, however, popular, with contributions made of whatever amount the guests felt they could offer. John took his family and never mentioned what he handed in. "It's nobody's business what I pay for my supper," he said.

Neither these pleasant encounters with non-Friends nor the smallness of the group of their own faith lessened the impact of Quaker thought on the growing Rushmore children. They always attended Quarterly Meeting when it was held in the nearby town of Quaker Street, and sometimes had the treat of going with their parents when it convened at Albany. Since the longer trip meant an all-day drive, their horses could not be burdened with too heavy a load, but for the child who was allowed to go for the three-day occasion, the big city and the crowd at Quarterly Meeting were high events. The visitors were always entertained with lavish hospitality, and social features then seemed more important to Jane than the meetings.

Although their father was such a strenuous follower of Elias Hicks, the children were never made aware of the split that had rent American Quakerism. They thought of themselves just as "the Friends." Jane was not conscious until she went to New York Yearly Meeting when she was twenty that any other branch existed. The parental wisdom that made no reference to divisions, the fortunate lack of contact with more heated city tempers—where children on one side of the line talked scornfully of the "Holy O's" and those on the other pointed fingers at their opposite numbers and said, "Poison! Poison!"—meant that this family had no bitterness to outgrow, and Jane in particular no hesitation when the time came for reconciling overtures.

To be sure Jane did not feast with pleasure on all the Quaker diet she was offered. When her father, with less pedagogic skill than his daughter later manifested, offered her five dollars to read George Fox's *Journal,* she announced after two chapters that she'd rather pull weeds to earn spending money. As a little child she was often reduced to counting the knotholes in the rafters of the meeting house while waiting for Grandfather Drake to break meeting. And when she was about twelve years old she heard a minister use the word "resurrection" a good deal in one of the family meetings for worship then often held. Jane took up the matter with the preacher at the close of the period of worship, asking quite specific questions about the body's walking after it was dead. She considered the replies evasive, indirect, and unsatisfactory.

Yet some of the visiting Friends left a deep impression. Always entertained at the Rushmore home, holding the small and intimate family meetings there, being driven to the regular or appointed gatherings in the meeting house, these guests from the outer reaches of Quakerdom were a real part of the children's lives. Jane remembers especially Thomas Foulke of New York, a great expositor of the Bible; John J. Cornell from Rochester, N. Y., who was an unimpassioned but clear-cut, logical interpreter of Hicksite views; and Margaretta Walton of London Grove, Pa. With no premonition of how close the association with Margaretta Walton and her family was to become, Jane looked with young admiration upon a strikingly handsome woman whose serene face took on added beauty from the most orthodox Quaker garb of that era, with its exquisitely made transparent white cap and immaculate sheer white kerchief folded down the front of a plain gray or black dress. Margaretta was an acceptable preacher wherever she went, for she spoke with deep feeling and a rather hortatory, pleading eloquence which her hearers found genuinely moving.

The succession of travelers passing through their home and the prized journeys to Quarterly Meeting were two of the main factors which maintained connection with the outside world of Quakerism. A third was the wide range of acquaintances made through Grandfather Drake. Israel Drake in the course of his wanderings had found various Friends who were looking for comfortable vacation quarters. He began to take them into his own home in summer as paying guests. To them he was a delightful host, driving them about the country in his three-seater, explaining local points of interest. Sometimes a single family took over one end of the large house completely, sometimes a group of friends made up a party and came together. Over the years this practice brought a good number of Friends into Potter Hollow. Among them were Dillwyn and Susan Parrish, important members of Race Street Meeting; Deborah Fisher Wharton, at one time clerk of the Women's Philadelphia Yearly Meeting; the Acton family, Elizabeth, Sarah, and their mother, from Salem, N. J.; and Edward Parrish, first president of Swarthmore College.

Jane and her brothers often spent a week or more at their grandfather's, which gave them a good opportunity to make friends with the visitors. After supper, family and guests gathered in the lamplight of the living room for conversation or reading aloud. The children were soon dismissed, but Jane's curiosity to know what the grownups talked about found a way to circumvent going to bed. The table had long drop leaves and a longer cloth over it. Under this excellent cover Jane sat, listening to the talk, enjoying the long words she did not always understand, and thrilling with the cadences and rhythm of "Hiawatha," read by one of the Acton sisters.

In this matrix of simple but stimulating living the five Rushmore children were prepared for emergence into a wider area of activity. Even as they grew up some hints of new conditions that the turn of the century would bring into American life were being heard. The high-wheel bicycles gave way to the "safety" variety, one of which nearly caused the end of Jane when she struck a stone as she coasted down a mountain road. Electric lights and telephones were beginning to make their appearance in large cities, though they had not reached remote country villages. It was still some time before a tale went through Preston Hollow that a carriage had been seen traveling along the road without horses. Many people did not believe the absurd rumor, setting it down as "one of those stage drivers' yarns."

But it was not to mechanical improvements that this family turned. Their lives reflected the patterns set in childhood. None of them, to be sure, stayed on the acres of their forebears; none of them became farmers. Charles, the eldest, became a dealer in wholesale provisions in Albany. Edward Cary, always bookish and intellectual, studied medicine and was for fifty years a beloved and honored physician in Tuxedo Park, N. Y., becoming chief of staff of its hospital. Mary also made a career of medicine and surgery until she broke her health in caring for poor patients. Anna married George Irwin and gave her attention to homemaking, a woman's club, and sharing her husband's many interests in Catskill, where they lived.

Of them all, Jane had perhaps the least indication as to where her brief training would lead her.

CHAPTER II

Sharpening the Tools

John Rushmore's intention was to give all his children a good education. To him, as to all rural families, this posed a problem. Small one- or two-room public schoolhouses were well distributed throughout the country, but facilities were necessarily meager for one teacher and a handful of children. School busses gathering pupils from a wide area and well-equipped union schools were far in the future. The Cooksburg public school was nearest to the Rushmores, and here Charles and Edward and Jane began, while their father ruminated on what better steps could be taken.

The first year of Jane's formal education cut two experiences deep into her memory. Her grandmother had knitted her some bright red stockings, and very pretty they must have been. None of the other girls had such gay ones, so they ridiculed her. She tried to keep her legs out of sight, but she had to pay the penalty of nonconformity until at last her brothers came to her rescue and stopped the persecution by pelting the other girls with acorns. Academically she ran into rough weather too. In the usual custom of that day Jane was to recite a poem (it was called "speaking a piece") before the school. When she found herself face to face with her audience for the first time she became so paralyzed with fear that she rushed back to her seat in tears. It was years before she forgot the fright of that moment or was able to vanquish its influence. Perhaps she might never have done so had her mother not insisted that she should not be excused, as the teacher was willing to do, but should take her turn again in proper course. When that time came she stood at a spot on the platform where the stove was between her and most of the school, fixed her eyes on a point in the stovepipe, and ran through the piece as fast as she could mutter the words. Those who knew her long after as a forceful, assured speaker may be surprised to learn that there were many later occasions when she longed for a stovepipe.

The Rushmore home supplemented the resources of the school with a moderate number of books, all eagerly devoured by the children. Edward read the whole of a bulky ancient history, several dull volumes, when he was seven. Even a new book put for safety on a high shelf he climbed up for and abstracted from time to time to read. But the problem of adequate regular schooling remained, and was increased by the determination of the parents that the two boys were not to be favored more than the three girls. Both the established Quaker principle of equality of the sexes and the Drake tradition supported similar training for all. So although the older children started in the rural public school, it was not long before their father planned for an improvement. He was the prime mover in setting up a private school, and for many years, while his children attended it, was its chief financial backer.

Miss Rose Hartwell, a lady of education and good manners, undertook this venture in a large second-floor room of her own home in Preston Hollow. There were perhaps a dozen pupils. Miss Hartwell gave all she had to her small flock, preparing the five Rushmores as well as she was able for a higher education. In addition Jane loved to read history with her Aunt Mary Drake, and her own natural gravitation toward books widened her knowledge of English literature.

SHARPENING THE TOOLS

Besides undergirding the private school, John Rushmore had made definite plans to put each of his children through college, a rather unusual ambition for his day, especially so far as girls were concerned. He had saved through the years a substantial sum for this purpose. Before it could be used, however, depreciation of his investments so reduced the amount that only two years of higher education could be allotted to each child.

Charles did not care to finish college; Edward was determined to graduate and then pursue the study of medicine, which he did by his own efforts. Jane followed her brothers to Swarthmore. Although she was not completely prepared, by hard work she passed off her conditions soon after she entered. That was in the autumn of 1878, before she was fifteen.

Swarthmore, like a number of older institutions which began as seminaries and afterwards raised their rank, was emerging from a status of preparatory school plus first college years and trying to shed its swaddling clothes to become exclusively a full-fledged college. All four undergraduate years were operating by 1878, but many of the regulations retained a strong flavor of boarding school. Undoubtedly these rules clung longer than they might otherwise have done because Swarthmore was coeducational and the conventions required very strict supervision of the girls. In the approved architecture of the day there was one large building to house the entire school. The boys' dormitory was at one end of the upper floors, the girls' at the other, with Collection Hall in the center. All lights were out at 10 P.M. By official regulation only Seniors and Juniors might use the front door. The girls must take their walks within strictly prescribed boundaries unless a teacher was along. The college proudly boasted two telephones, one in the president's office and one in the superintendent's. Any student who had never used this instrument might go to the superintendent's office, speak to the station agent a quarter of a mile away, and hear his reply. Jane was delighted to avail herself of the opportunity.

On entering Swarthmore, Jane had not had sufficient preliminary Latin, a subject she did not like or see any sense in. She and three other girls who were all having the same difficulty thought up a plan of writing to their fathers to see if they could not be excused from the course. Jane wrote eloquently on how foolish it was to spend her time on such a subject. Much better to have the extra time for English; Latin was of no practical use and she couldn't do it anyway. The last phrase was a mistake. John Rushmore replied that if she really could not learn Latin he understood there was another institution farther up the road where she could go, and she'd better take the train. His daughter did not have to be told that he was referring to the Elwyn School for the feeble-minded.

Instruction tactics were for the professor to tell the students what they ought to know or to give them an assignment in a book, and then for the students to tell the information back to the professor. This method, while out of date today, had its uses. The history course under Maria L. Sanford, for example, comprising a deluge of dates, persons, places, and events, Jane found valuable many years later when she became an addict to crossword puzzles.

There was a Sunday custom which Miss Sanford encouraged—a recitation of Bible verses just before the opening of the meeting for worship. Miss Sanford so strongly approved the idea that she gave extra credit in her courses to those who thus participated in public worship, and if a student happened to be one who was good in history and had answered all the class questions correctly, his mark would run above 100, although 100 was the most that could go on his record. Jane, however, was not one of those who volunteered with Bible texts.

If the methods of teaching were old-fashioned, nevertheless there were personalities among the faculty who made a lasting impression on Jane. Edward Magill, the president, a man of vigorous intellect, was engaged in a hard pioneering struggle to raise academic standards. It was uphill work to impress some of his Board with the difference between a school and a college, but his mental brisk step, like his physical one, carried him forward. Already that remarkable woman, Susan J. Cunningham, was on the staff, teaching mathematics, but it was for her down-to-earth good judgment that Jane still remembers her, calling her "professor of gumption and common sense." The astronomical observatory was built for her later.

William Hyde Appleton, with the mind and temperament of a true scholar, instilled into many college generations a love of learning; Samuel S. Green, the absent-minded professor, delighted his class by inquiring plaintively, "Does anybody know where my laboratory keys are?" while jingling them in his hand. Promising boys were being attracted to the college by a comparatively young, nearsighted man, Arthur Beardsley, who with the most modest equipment was turning out good engineers and was laying the sound foundations for the present excellent department of engineering. Maria Sanford herself, later head of the Department of Rhetoric at the University of Minnesota, became so well known there that she was called "Minnesota's Grand Old Lady."

UNDER QUAKER APPOINTMENT

There were some notable visiting professors. The famous Dr. Joseph Leidy came out from the University of Pennsylvania to teach natural history (biology). He did not care much for examinations, but when he had to give them he turned the papers over to be marked by a young Swarthmore teacher, Edward Martin, afterward a prominent surgeon and for a time head of the Department of Health for Philadelphia. And Dr. Joseph Thomas, physician and lexicographer, came once or twice a week to lecture on English literature.

With the Swarthmore students drawn largely from the Hicksite body of Friends, Jane's acquaintance in this group widened to include those from more distant Meetings. Perhaps the Moore family from Sandy Spring, Md., was her first direct touch with the South. It was certainly a fairly extensive sampling, for besides Esther, who was on the faculty, there were among Jane's fellow students Mary, Tom, Joe, Fred, George, and Roland, all closely related. Thanks to her mother's early friendship, Jane spent one of her college vacations at the home of Charles and Hannah Marot in Philadelphia, where one day a neighbor's child of about four came in, running to a blackboard to draw pictures. Soon the family began to suggest objects to him, and anything they mentioned he could draw. His facility was so unusual that Jane remembered his name. It was Maxfield Parrish, who years later was the nationally known illustrator.

Of all the subjects Jane studied, English was her favorite. She enjoyed doing her best in the writing of her themes. One assignment was a description of a storm. She had watched many furious tempests spend their strength in the Catskill Mountains as she grew up; they belonged to the fabric of a country child's life, where weather was an important part in the economy of the neighborhood. So Jane wrote her theme out of experience and feeling. The result was so good that the instructor asked what she had copied it from. "From nature!" replied the indignant author. Then and there Jane determined that all her writing should be as effective as she could possibly make it. One of her classmates especially appreciated her gift in this field, a girl from Virginia who had money but considerably less talent in English. She proposed to give Jane a dozen bananas if she would write her essay for her. Jane felt no scruple whatever about accepting this excellent bargain, which goes to show that standards of academic probity vary and are not to be confused with desire for recognition of an accomplishment that is one's own.

Besides developing her skill of clear and original expression, Jane was also absorbing the information of her choice with remarkable retentiveness and understanding. Her procedure was shown in an incident that occurred some years after she left Swarthmore when she was taking a special course in mathematics at the University of Pennsylvania. The teacher had been demonstrating a problem in trigonometry when he noticed that this student was not copying the demonstration as the others were. "Where are your notes?" he demanded. Jane pointed to her head. While the man was considering this unlikely situation, Jane went on to remark, indicating the figures set forth, "I understand you up to this point. After that I do not follow you." Forced to return his attention to the blackboard the professor went through the explanation again, stopped at the place Jane had signified, and had to admit that he had made an error. All her life, beginning with the Swarthmore classrooms, Jane has filled no notebooks and kept no files, but has depended completely on an alert and disciplined memory. It is a way too hard for most students, but for her the result has been an elasticity and tenacity which have never weakened through the years.

Such a technique of learning produced good results in Jane's self-appointed explorations. The college library was a mine of wealth which fascinated her. She never knew there were so many books, although the library was actually very small at the time. She couldn't stay away from these freely accessible riches, reading two or three books a week, sometimes to the detriment of regular work. Perhaps the library gave her a better grounding of education than the classrooms, for through it she developed a reading habit and further trained her excellent memory.

Other extracurricular incidents had their share of influence in Jane's brief two years. One was a visit to the college by Lucretia Mott, then near the end of her long life. A Nantucket-born Quaker, she and her husband James had been ardent workers for the emancipation of the slaves. Later with Elizabeth Cady Stanton she turned her attention particularly to women's rights, although temperance and universal peace also shared her interest. While she was inescapably a reformer throughout her career, the impression she made on young Jane Rushmore was far from that of a stern ax-wielder. The little old lady, frail and delicate, in her eighties, was gifted with no especial eloquence. But she gave to her youthful listener a curious feeling of an entirely different atmosphere, a sense of an invisible aura, very much like that which Jane experienced years later in the presence of Tagore, in each case sensing a personality upheld by the power of spiritual forces.

Quite different was the effect of an invitation to visit Deborah Fisher Wharton. Jane knew this lady to be very wealthy, and the prospect of seeing a millionaire's home was alluring. To her great surprise she was welcomed to a house plainer and simpler than her father's. For the first time it dawned on her that plainness really meant something. If a woman who had a million dollars found it actually undesirable to buy the superfluities she might have had, then those things were not necessary for anyone. Jane never again cared whether or not she had things of her own that other people had. The Quaker principle of simplicity had come alive for her.

In 1878 Swarthmore was not an important college. Its scholarship, in spite of President Magill's efforts, scarcely had a glimpse of the high plane it was to reach half a century later. But its set of values for living was very fine. Of her short stay there, Jane did not even take full college work the first year. Yet from her Swarthmore experience she received a totally different approach to life, a new sense of a bigger world and something to be done in it. No educator can ask more than this for his labors.

Jane also found at Swarthmore a new idea of what a Quaker Meeting could be. Composed of students (who were required to attend), faculty, and the few families who were the nucleus of the village later to thrive around the college, it was far larger than any local Meeting she had ever attended. Its many visitors came from a rather different sphere, and the meetings for worship were often stimulating, encouraging, and vital. Jane became personally interested in being a Friend.

When at the end of two years she went home, she continued her education by correspondence courses. In the next three years she worked with the Boston Society for Home Study. She had just one correspondent teacher with whom she took all her courses: history, economics, and literature. The work was very thorough, each subject a possible equivalent to a year's course in the same field in college.

In 1882 she was appointed to teach the Preston Hollow Public School, ungraded, with forty pupils who were in such a state of disorder that they had already ousted two teachers. Jane took stock of her rather forbidding first job. She found that there were three big boys who really wanted to learn. They walked with her to school, and they took over the troublemakers. They administered discipline on the school grounds by other than approved pedagogic methods, but effectively enough so that the wayward found it easier to come along with the teacher's ideas than face the strong-arm squad outside. Jane had not been able to obtain a New York State first-grade certificate before she started teaching because she had had no experience. At New Year's, when she was turning nineteen, it was granted to her because of her success in subduing that school. Of course the boys deserved the certificate, she said later. She kept in touch with them for years afterward. All of them turned out well.

After watching the new teacher at Preston Hollow, the parents of the three boys decided to establish another private school in the village with Jane as the teacher. The one she herself had attended had closed when there were no more Rushmore children to support it. The new school was set up over the general store. Among the ten or fifteen pupils was one unprepossessing lad whom Jane was warned not to accept because his family would not pay the tuition. She decided to take him. Sure enough, there was no response whatever to the bill. Jane's salary depended on the tuition payments and she drew a blank in this case. About ten years later when she had left New York, Jane one day received an envelope containing the original statement, yellow with age, a check in full with compound interest added, and a note explaining that the young man was now in a position to pay his debts.

At the close of the brief school year, eight months in farming communities, Jane gave herself a little trip away from home. Since going to Swarthmore she had developed some taste for the outside world, so she went to New York City for her first Yearly Meeting late in May 1884.

She knew that the men's and women's business sessions would be held separately. As she sat with the women, she found some impressive figures. There, wearing a plain scoop bonnet, was Phoebe Anna Thorne, who later gave the money to establish a model school in connection with Bryn Mawr College. There, too, was Hannah W. Haydock, a woman also greatly interested in education, a member of the first Board of Managers of Swarthmore College and one of the founders of the first medical school in New York open to women. She was among those who kept open house during Yearly Meeting for all visiting Friends. Another hostess was Jane Russell, who observed great plainness in dress but did not carry this simplicity to her ornate and apparently elaborately staffed home. Every day during Yearly Meeting a smart pair of horses with liveried coachman waited with the carriage to take Friends home to a plentiful dinner, served by a colored waiter. Jane Rushmore, still rather unsophisticated, enjoyed this extensive hospitality as a marked feature of the week. Marianna Chapman, whom Jane thought the handsomest woman in the Yearly Meeting, was chairman of the Epistle Committee and very active in all Meeting affairs, while Phoebe C. Wright, little, plain, and not impressive at all, took a serious responsibility in a number of civic matters, especially in seeing that matrons were installed in police stations where women prisoners were sent.

As a promising young Friend, Jane was at once given a job at Yearly Meeting—that of serving on the Epistle Committee for the Women's Meeting. It was the custom to write a separate epistle to each Yearly Meeting with whom they corresponded. To accomplish this, each member of the committee took one of the incoming letters to answer. Jane accepted one, wrote her reply, and presented it to the committee when it met. In the approved manner of such gatherings, commendation was expressed, and various polite suggestions were made. At the end only one sentence of the original was left, and the Yearly Meeting in session took that out. Her mother and some of the committee felt very sorry. But Jane said, "Oh, we have a barrel of old ones at home in the printed *Extracts,* and I can write one just like them." So the next year she did, with all the well-worn, familiar phrases, and it was admired. But she never wrote another.

Well-known Quaker preachers were in attendance, some of whom Jane had heard before but whose words were more impressive in the large joint meeting for worship. Sunderland P. Gardiner, a visitor from Genesee (Canada), spoke rapidly with well-chosen words as he walked up and down the length of the gallery unless, as Jane was not slow to notice, someone put out a foot to bar his progress. He often even loosened his necktie to relieve the tension of speaking. The constant theme of these impassioned discourses was the conviction that God speaks directly to those who seek Him, and through the Bible importantly but secondarily. Another Genesee Friend present at these sessions was Isaac Wilson, fluent and able, who often stressed the thought that sin was not hereditary, but original with him who commits it, and who believed that resurrection was a spiritual and not a physical phenomenon. Both of these men were typical Hicksites.

In the membership of New York Meeting were a number of men who were prominent for various reasons, and whom Jane now met for the first time. Joseph A. Bogardus, a strong temperance advocate, served on committees for many other good causes as well; Aaron M. Powell, cultured and persuasive, was chiefly associated with the campaign for "Social and Moral Prophylaxis," and was the brother of Elizabeth Powell Bond who was later dean of Swarthmore College; John W. Hutchinson was very active in penal reform movements. William M. Jackson, Jane observed, was one of the rather rare group who seemed to think twice before he spoke once. His wife, Anna M. Jackson, was devoted to the cause of education for the newly freed Negroes, particularly to support of the Laing School in Aiken, S. C. She never tired of keeping its needs before all whom she could reach, and the early struggles to offer educational opportunities to colored people owe much to her. This group of Friends gave leadership in a wide range of social reform movements. It was their deep belief that religion should be translated into the raising of the whole community nearer to the Christian ideal.

Another of their number was Henry W. Wilbur, a very gifted man. A clear and forceful speaker, author of a life of Elias Hicks and of other shorter studies, he later became the first executive secretary of the Advancement Committee. One of his convictions, often stated, was that "the most important thing in life is to build life." His great native ability and vigorous personality were somewhat hampered by lack of early opportunity, yet he became a real leader in the wide field of the Friends General Conference.

There were younger Friends of Jane's own age at Yearly Meeting whose acquaintance was to last over many years. They included Elizabeth Stover, afterwards co-principal of Brooklyn Friends School, Josephine Tilton, a future recording secretary of Friends General Conference, Esther Haviland Cornell and her husband, Edward Cornell, whose later career embraced being a successful corporation lawyer, clerk of New York Yearly Meeting, and superintendent of the Brooklyn First-day School, and Harry A. Hawkins, the hardest and busiest worker Jane ever saw, but one never in the limelight.

Perhaps, however, the most important person to Jane at that 1884 New York Yearly Meeting was Lavinia Yeatman, a visitor from Pennsylvania. She was not of outstanding fame, but she was a good observer, and she carried in her mind the need of filling an open position at home. During the week she approached Jane and asked if she would like to take charge of the London Grove Friends School, thirty miles out of Philadelphia. Jane promised to think it over. She went home, considered the proposal, and wrote for further information, enclosing her treasured first-grade certificate and giving as references the names of Margaretta Walton and Deborah

Wharton. If the committee was satisfied, she would be glad to accept the appointment. A letter in reply stated that in view of the character of the references no further correspondence would be necessary.

During the summer Jane prepared to leave Preston Hollow. The new school she would teach was no larger than the one she was relinquishing, which was forthwith closed. Nor was the new salary any special inducement. But she was going to a new place, nearer to large cities, nearer to the locality she had known when she was at Swarthmore. It was an adventure to take a job away from home. So she packed her small trunk and set forth to her first employment within the circuit of Philadelphia Yearly Meeting. She was twenty years old.

CHAPTER III

"Jane, Chester County, Pa."

Jane Rushmore's observant blue eyes were quick in their survey of the scene of her new activities. She found that, in contrast to the rural locality where she had grown up, the Friends were the majority in numbers and influence. The London Grove Meeting was large. Its members, mostly farmers, of course, were well educated and prosperous. They identified themselves as being "from Chester County," partly because Bayard Taylor, the author, Ezra Michener, who in 1860 wrote a *Retrospect of Early Quakerism,* and John Bartram and Humphrey Marshall, the naturalists, all were born there, partly from a certain pride in their direct descent from the founding settlers. Friends had established themselves in London Grove early in the eighteenth century; their original log meeting house was built in 1714. Names of the first trustees of the grant were still perpetuated in their descendants, whose fertile acres spread widely around the big stone house of worship and the small village.

The school was Jane's immediate concern, so she was pleased to discover that London Grove Friends were interested in education. Some of them believed that they should patronize the public school and lend their support to its improvement. Others felt that the best environment for their children was a school under the care of the Meeting. But they had had some trouble in maintaining a private school. Its stone building had been erected by Friends in 1818, directly across the road from the meeting house. Then financial difficulty had developed an odd situation. The ground floor was rented to the public school, while the second floor was used for the Meeting's school. Fortunately there was no animosity between the educational rivals. In the single room upstairs can still be seen the teacher's platform all the way across one end, with blackboards behind it, and, at the other end, small alcoves for the boys' and girls' wraps, closets for books and equipment, and a tall secretary-bookcase filled with dusty mineral specimens. The last were not much used, but in a small school with few resources such a collection, doubtless given by a neighborhood amateur geologist, had its value on rainy days.

At the opening in the autumn of 1884, twelve children appeared. Jane was, of course, the one teacher. She was not dismayed at the small size of the enrollment nor at the modest salary of $40 a month (later increased to $50 when the school did well); after all she had been taught and had done a year's teaching in just such small schools. It did not take her long, however, to see a difference here. In Preston Hollow private education was almost in the nature of tutoring groups, enduring while the most interested families kept them up, then disappearing. But the London Grove School had a history of more than sixty years, whose lapses in continuity—doubtless there had been some—were the temporary feature rather than the existence itself. London Grove was an even smaller hamlet than the ones of Jane's childhood, but the surrounding country was full of Friends' families. Here were real potentialities for growth if she could be persuasive enough. She liked challenges.

From the beginning it was obvious that she would find great reliance and strength in Robert L. Pyle. He was a member of the school committee; some of his children were already among the first twelve. He was a small man, growing deaf, who had begun his career as a country storekeeper. His ability developed the business into a merchandizing establishment to which people drove from miles around. Later three branch stores were set up in towns some distance away. He became president of the First National Bank of West Grove. To his acumen were added fair dealing and interest in people. Never swallowed up in business, he was always ready to help in neighborhood affairs, with a singular capacity for getting things done. He seldom appeared in a public position; usually someone else sat in the chairman's seat. But it was his finely balanced reasoning, his intelligent grasp, and his careful attention that made him a mainstay not only in his own family but throughout the community. Jane discovered this early, and she watched through many years his strong, reliable judgment functioning in the guidance of her school, in London Grove Meeting, and in the most important committees of the Yearly Meeting.

Hospitality was characteristic of the Pyles. Soon after Jane's arrival in London Grove she was invited there to supper, and the youngest son, Robert, embarked on a tale of his latest exploit in gathering chestnuts. Each of his crowd of boys was working to see who could get a bushel first. Robert was ahead and well pleased about it. They planned to thrash the trees the next day. The new teacher listened as they sat in front of the fire. Then she said, "Well, whose chestnuts are these?" Her small auditor was astonished. Weren't chestnuts the possession of any seven-year-old who found them? That evening, Robert said years later, he had his first lesson in property rights. The next day's expedition was abandoned.

At first Jane lived in the home of David and Emmaline Swayne, where she remembers a surprise party given her on her twenty-first birthday. She walked in from school to a room full of people who evidently felt rather warmly already toward the new teacher so recently come among them. The following year she moved to the house of Dr. Joseph Stubbs, whose wife Deborah was to be a close and congenial friend as long as she lived.

Before her marriage Deborah Walton had been a teacher at Darlington Seminary in West Chester. She was cultured, quiet, and dignified. When Jane, soon after her arrival, stirred the London Grove Meeting up to starting a First-day school, Deborah Stubbs at once became active in it. Later she was a member of Ministers and Elders for the Meeting. As the wife of a busy country doctor and the mother of two children she was little away from home, though there was a great deal of company at the house. She was, however, appointed a member of the first committee on George School, helping to set the stamp on its earliest years and making a connection destined to be of importance to herself. She was always interested in reading, including not only new books as they came out, but the classics. She proposed to Jane that they read Latin together. Accordingly they spent some time with Cicero and Virgil, Jane having fortunately recovered from her earlier antipathy to the old language. Deborah expressed herself well on questions of national life, or local affairs as these were discussed by the two women and Dr. Stubbs, and the ladies found each other mutually stimulating.

The Stubbs house was a scant mile from the school. In all weathers Jane could be seen swinging down the lane and up the road to the schoolhouse in a steady stride. Only once did she fail to open the school. That was after a blizzard when the drifts in the road were so high that the horse driven by Dr. Stubbs's man was stuck beyond any possibility of getting through.

"JANE, CHESTER COUNTY, PA."

For perhaps four or five years she conducted the school alone. Some of her moves, it was true, had been looked at askance by at least a few Friends. When their school had an outside speaker or a special demonstration, financed by the Yearly Meeting's Committee on Education, Jane had invited the children from downstairs to come in. She was rebuked by the timid, who remonstrated, "What's the use of a private school if its advantages are to be shared with public-school children?" But Jane was right. She was making friends and practising democracy.

While some questions came up that had to be decided by the committee, and some on which Jane sought the counsel of Robert L. Pyle or other committee members, there were some matters which she dealt with unhesitatingly. It never occurred to her to ask for a committee decision about accepting colored children. These little boys and girls were used to coming to the downstairs school when it was public; now when a few of them applied under the new dispensation they were accepted. Earlier there had been an older boy who wanted to be prepared for Lincoln University. Israel Drake's granddaughter did not consider refusing him; she only suggested that he sit at the end of the bench and leave the girls alone. There was no tornado at London Grove. Everything went as calmly as ever with no objections raised. It was a matter of course.

The pupils began on her arrival to address her as Teacher Jane. Among Friends it was not the custom to use the worldly appellations of Mr., Mrs., or Miss, and these children were practising an accepted substitute. The new incumbent, scarcely older than some of her students, did not care for the title, so she had the boys and girls call her Jane from the start. As her acquaintance widened rapidly through the entire neighborhood, she was always named in the same way. Some years later a Philadelphia Friend remarked that if a letter addressed to "Jane, Chester County, Pa." were posted he was sure it would reach her.

As she left Preston Hollow to go to London Grove, her father had offered her a parting admonition: "Remember, you will not be important to the community until you make yourself so." Jane therefore undertook to build herself into Chester County. She attended the local teachers' institutes and the farmers' institutes. The latter made a practice of always having a woman on the program. Before long Jane was invited to this place. The first year she refused, saying she didn't know anything about jellies and cakes. The next time she consented, speaking on "The Farmer of the Future." She thought that safe since no one knows anything about the future. She did touch on the condition of the roads, then almost hub deep in mud. She decried it as foolish to haul dirt to fill in the roads, then haul it out as mud on wagon wheels so that the they could haul in more dirt. "What do you know about road building?" someone called out. "I'm no expert on building roads, I'm only an expert on how not to build them," she replied. On another occasion, with taxation as her subject, she held that the farmer is doubly taxed. First he pays interest on the mortgage because he can't pay for the farm, and then he pays taxes because he's the owner of it. Her remarks, both apt and quaint, caught the fancy of the average farmer and her papers were always popular.

Quite different were the teachers' institutes, which she attended for professional help. After Joseph S. Walton, brother of Deborah Stubbs, was elected county superintendent by the school directors, he changed the character of the institutes so that the best available instruction was given. Of course they were set up for the benefit of the teachers in the public schools, but they were open to anyone who wanted to be present. Adhering to her established practice, Jane took no notes at the sessions. She said she was afraid of getting into a rut, teaching the same thing the same way time after time. Ruts are comfortable, but you can't grow in them. You only grow to them.

Other ruts than teaching ones offended Jane too. When she first came to the three-day institute she observed that most of the teachers wore a different dress every day. She did not propose to do anything of that sort. She was able to keep a dress clean for a few days. So she took only one, and at the first meal a waitress spilled a whole dish of sticky preserve down her shoulder and sleeve. She remarked, "Now I know how it feels to be stuck up," and after that she brought along an extra frock.

Ultimately she herself became an almost constant speaker at the local institutes, either formally or informally, where her remarks were related to the immediate situation, sensible and cogent, and always laced with humor and witty phrasing.

Whatever Jane may have learned at the institutes, the quality of her teaching must have been largely her own. Here was a one-room, one-teacher school at its best. Robert Pyle, among her earliest pupils, recalled that she sat at an angle to her desk, her left elbow resting on it, her right hand slowly sliding the little gold charm on her long watch chain. The reciting class took the seats immediately in front of her. Other children were supposedly doing their own tasks behind. When the recitation began, however, it frequently happened that all the children stopped their work, engrossed in listening to Jane. She analyzed everything to the bottom. Explanations were within the child's grasp and so thorough they were unforgettable. Side issues were discussed if they were brought up. The ranging interest and the unconventional treatment of the subjects made many of the classes a miniature forum for the entire school. The teacher had great understanding, a remarkable power of insight, and she was just. These qualities made discipline almost unnecessary. At least no one remembers instances of it now, except a few in midweek meeting.

A meeting for worship was regularly held on one of the mornings in the middle of the week by all Friends at this time, and if there was a local Friends' school, the children invariably attended. On Wednesday mornings at London Grove the children walked quietly, not in formation but in natural groups, across the road and into the meeting house, boys sitting on the men's side, girls on the women's. Although these children were in great proportion Friends, accustomed to silent worship, yet when a large group sat together it was pretty hard not to give way to giggles or a little mischief. Once when there was some disturbance on the boys' side, Jane rose from her seat with the girls and ushered the offender to the facing bench where the whole meeting had its eye on him. "The only time I was ever invited to sit in the gallery," the culprit said years later.

A boy had been told one day to finish a piece of work before he went home, but instead he started to leave. Jane backed up to the only door and said to him, "Thee can go if thee wants to, but I would like thee to think about something first. If thee goes, which thee may do, thee will never come back. Think it over." He stood twisting his cap for a long minute, then set down his dinner pail. "What do you want me to do?" he grumbled. When he finished in about five minutes, his good temper restored, Jane said cheerfully, "Goodbye, I'll be very glad to see thee tomorrow."

Many of her pupils now recall how thoughtfully and carefully she went over their problems with them, how little discipline was ever apparent, and they repeatedly say, "She was a wonderful teacher!" One of them, who later reached a place of considerable prominence, tells with amusement that he said to her fervently in his mature years, "Everything I ever amounted to I owe to thee." "Oh, don't mention a little thing like that," Jane replied absently.

Naturally enough, the vigorous head of their school became a person of note in the Monthly Meeting. Almost immediately after her arrival in London Grove a large temperance meeting was held, at which antislavery, a crusade successfully concluded two decades earlier, was constantly referred to as a parallel cause. The uninhibited newcomer entered into a debate on this issue then and there, declaring that here were two basically different questions and that it was muddy thinking to bracket them together. London Grove sat up. What was this young firecracker they had invited to their midst?

At that time the local Young Friends Association was an active organization whose program was that of a literary society. Some of their meetings were given over to debates, which had a great vogue around the nineties. Jane enjoyed these very much and was often on one of the teams until it grew difficult to find anyone to oppose her. Her plan was to think up all her opponent's points and rebut them before he had a chance to speak.

She did not have, fortunately, so devastating an effect in the many First-day school and Friends Association conferences that were held jointly with other such groups from a wider area. In these cheerful, sociable assemblies, again she took sufficient part to be noticed, because she was shortly asked to read a paper one evening of Yearly Meeting Week in Philadelphia when the First-day School Committee had charge of the program. The headliner that night was Jesse H. Holmes, whose explosive force always drew a large crowd. It was a warm May evening, and Jane wore a light, summery dress which, with her blond hair, gave her a very youthful aspect. The presiding officer opened the meeting and in due time called for Jane. As she rose and walked down the aisle, he looked at her without recognition and said, as if bored by an interruption, "What does thee want?" "Nothing in particular," Jane said, "I was just answering to my name." "Oh," blurted the surprised chairman, "I was expecting thee to be middle-aged, dark, and strong-minded looking."

London Grove offered more than Quakerly activities, grange meetings, and teachers' institutes. The county seat, West Chester, only thirteen miles away, was a town which drew lecturers of wide reputation. These were the days of "University Extension" courses, which brought George W. Cable, James Whitcomb Riley, Thomas Wentworth Higginson, and other such celebrities of the time to outlying centers. To listen to these men was a great treat to Jane, who went to hear them as often as possible. The cultural opportunities of West Chester, by no means inconsiderable and greater than any she had had before except during her two years at college, were a prized addition to her education and brought her in touch with the outside world as she could not otherwise have been.

Two homes in London Grove were the center of her social life, that of Robert L. Pyle with his children (his wife had died), and that of Thomas Chalkley Bartram. Chalkley Bartram was treasurer of the school committee, his two children, Frank and Mary, were in the school, and his wife, Anna, was a great entertainer. Anniversaries of all kinds and holidays provided occasions for parties at the Bartrams, and the near conjunction of several birthdays, among them Jane's, meant that for years there was always high festivity in January at these houses. "We wrote poems to each other and ate a great succession of desserts," said Jane.

Although these were the families whom she visited most often, she of course knew everybody. As there were no trained nurses in the country, neighbors came in to help when illness or misfortune beset a household. Jane took her turn sitting up with the sick, only specifying that she must serve at the end of the week. To further her acquaintance with her pupils she stayed overnight in seemingly innumerable homes. It was a pretty taxing addition to her week's work, but she got to know the children well. In her mind this acquaintance was basic to sound teaching. She became, according to her own account, an expert on the comfort of beds in Chester County.

It was quite a step when because of increased enrollment the committee asked the public-school board to give up its downstairs room. Not only would the Friends not have the rent, but they would have to provide the salary of a teacher to take care of the elementary grades that were to be given the ground floor. However, the school was obviously prospering and the London Grove Meeting had confidence in the new venture. Thenceforth children were accepted for their whole elementary and secondary education. For a decade or more Jane headed a two-teacher school.

To conduct the elementary department Jane had had a succession of assistant teachers. For a variety of reasons none of them had stayed very long. By the spring of 1898 it became necessary to look again for an occupant of this position. The Committee on Education of Philadelphia Yearly Meeting, spearheaded by the stirring Clement M. Biddle of Lansdowne, had established a Friends' teacher-training class, to encourage Friends to go into teaching and to equip the students better for doing so. The class met every day in the Race Street Meeting House under Belle Mooney. During the course she took them for two weeks to Wilmington to observe the good Friends' school there, and again similarly to George School. The members of the class were given practice teaching by acting as substitutes in the various Friends' schools, and at the end of the year they knew something about their profession. So Jane came to Yearly Meeting in the spring of '98 to shop for a new assistant. Clement Biddle indicated one member of the training class whom he considered suitable, but the young woman seemed rather colorless to Jane and her eye roved further. "Well," said Clement, "there are some others over yonder," pointing to where a group of these girls stood together. "Bring me that one with the brown eyes and curly hair," said Jane, and was shortly introduced to Emma Barnes Wallace. Emma was engaged on the spot. She came to London Grove in the autumn to begin not only her teaching but a lifetime of the closest personal friendship with her associate.

Jane never regretted her choice. It was remarkable that Emma from the first never had any trouble with discipline in a situation that some of her predecessors had found difficult. She was young, pretty, shy, and gentle, characteristics that made people overlook her quite firm chin.

"JANE, CHESTER COUNTY, PA."

While the first qualities broke down the defenses, the chin marched in to victory without anyone's quite knowing what had happened. Emma was a success with the elementary grades on the first floor.

The whole school, indeed, had become a flourishing institution, favorably known all over the county. By 1900 it had grown in size to fifty-two, practically capacity for the two rooms. It had prepared students to enter Swarthmore and had sent out two others who after only one more year of further study had entered Smith and Cornell. Jane had made an ineradicable impression on the pupils she taught. Her school was definitely a Friends' school. Every morning the opening feature was a brief religious talk to the whole group of children. There was a reading from the Bible with explanation or background or comment from Jane, and then the core of the thought written on the blackboard for memorizing. This was no routine exercise; it had vitality and meaning. A number of her students still mention the sharp memory they retain of those talks on the Bible.

With no training in pedagogy, she used methods formulated years later by progressive schools. Quite unaware of what was developed long afterward as the Dalton plan, she gave the children individual assignments to work out. Each pupil wrote a composition every day on something he was interested in—only occasionally were topics given. Children and teachers together made a few rules so that they might have conditions in which they did not disturb each other. In the monthly report books prepared for parents the item of deportment was marked up by the children after they had consulted among themselves, and Jane found the boys and girls harder on offenders than she would have been.

There were special holidays given each year: in the winter a half-day for skating, in the spring a half-day for a picnic, and, best of all, a special party before Christmas for candy-making. Here the hospitable Bartram home appeared as a strong ally. Anna Bartram never minded how many children were tearing through her house, and the management of the occasion was assumed by her housekeeper, Mary Mackereth, a skilled candy artificer, and Jane. When it was over, each child had a box of sweets to carry home.

Another feature of the school year was a play. Jane had certainly had little theatrical experience, and plays were a novelty in Quaker schools then, to say the least, but she managed a satisfactory production. Some boys who wouldn't study were found to be excellent at the mechanics of staging.

As her own proficiency increased, Jane developed the potentialities not only of her students, but of her assistant. The school had a midday recess of a full hour. Jane and Emma carried their lunch to school, in pleasant weather sitting on the big stone step to eat it. During that lunch period Emma brought her problems to Jane and had, as she said, an hour of teacher training every day. To be taught by a woman of such ability was a priceless opportunity for a young beginner. Emma was learning how to apply what Jane stated in her speeches at institutes: that first you have to have knowledge of what you are going to teach, then you have to have knowledge of human nature and the individuality of your pupils, and finally you must have a technique for bringing your own knowledge into a form suitable to the human material before you.

Jane undoubtedly had a touch of genius in following this plan herself. In her classes everything moved forward enlivened by her original, offhand remarks. A certain

JANE P. RUSHMORE
(about 1900)

"JANE, CHESTER COUNTY, PA."

lame boy was disheartened by his handicap because it cut him off from athletic pursuits. Years later he came into the office at 1515 Cherry Street, bringing Jane a basket of fine peaches he had grown, explaining that now he was a successful accountant, and asked her if she remembered saying to him, "A man's ability to get on does not reside in his legs." Another pupil has stated that in caliber she ranked with the great Quaker educators like Benjamin F. Hallowell and Edward H. Magill and would have taken her place with them if she had worked in a larger field. None are more grateful to her than some of the boys who later became highly successful in their careers, such as Robert Pyle, president of the Conard Pyle Company, rose growers, and George Scarlett, state senator.

As the unusual quality of the teaching at London Grove became known through Chester County, other schools cast an appraising eye on its staff. Only five miles away, at Kennett Square, Martin Academy had a good reputation. It was under the care of Kennett Monthly Meeting, though it had received its name and some endowment funds from Samuel Martin, one of the Kennett Friends. In 1900 the committee of this school invited Jane Rushmore to become its principal and Emma Wallace to head the intermediate department. The school was much larger than the one where they had worked so long and its high-school department had gained considerable importance. Kennett Square was a town of fair size, indeed it was on the railroad, which meant that travel to other points was possible without a three-mile carriage drive to the station. Changes, moreover, had come about in living conditions at London Grove. After a serious break in the health of Dr. Stubbs a couple of years before, his wife had taken him to California, where the family lived for the short remaining period of his life. Jane Rushmore and Emma Wallace were naturally not so firmly rooted afterwards as they had been in the unusually congenial Stubbs home, a household Jane had shared for fourteen years. Perhaps they had been in one school long enough. New conditions were stimulating. They accepted the invitation.

In her new school the principal put into operation the methods which had been successfully tried out at London Grove. These included a considerable amount of student participation in school government, a drastic reduction in the number of formal rules, and lesson assignments calculated to stir up original thinking rather than the memorizing of factual knowledge. Teachers College of Columbia University was at this time advocating such changes in educational philosophy, but Jane was not acquainted with the fact that others were developing similar ideas for school management. She used her own commonsense view of what schools ought to try to do.

Like the rest of the Martin Academy staff, the new members lived, at least for the first year, at the Friends Home. But Jane soon grew to feel that the teachers unwittingly tended to dominate conditions at the Home, pushing the older residents into the background. She was glad when an opportunity came for her and Emma to become a part of Charles Pennock's family. They were already well acquainted. The three children were in the school and their mother was secretary of its Committee. Charles Pennock was a state ornithologist for Delaware, and birds became at once a subject of detailed interest to the newcomers in the household.

Social life in Kennett was quite different from that in London Grove. There was not the gathering in of all the community for a birthday party. Instead there were separate church groups, a large woman's club, and endless card-playing afternoons and evenings. The teachers at Martin

"JANE, CHESTER COUNTY, PA."

Academy did not want to play cards, since some of the patrons of the school disapproved such recreation. This withdrawal of the faculty members detached them from the town circles. When they did come to a party some other entertainment had to be devised for them. A few supporters of the school and all the teachers stood out against a card-ridden life, for it had become a community problem. But their efforts to reduce or change it were not very successful.

Kennett, however, had the great advantage of making Philadelphia accessible. Now, even more than in earlier years, Jane and Emma were constantly going somewhere on Saturdays—to institutes, conferences, classes at the University of Pennsylvania. Jane was in ever greater demand as a speaker and she could now more easily reach the larger gatherings at Fifteenth and Race streets. Without her being in the least conscious of it, Jane's interest was being bit by bit weaned away from schoolwork.

Her program was much more strenuous than before. The larger, graded school with definite requirements for graduation made a heavier administrative load, and the teaching had to be somewhat more formal. It was not possible on account of the size of the school to have quite the same relationship with the individual pupils, though Jane did her best. She was pleased that from her first small graduating class Howard Thomas won a Haverford College scholarship and Philip M. Hicks the I. V. Williamson partial scholarship to Swarthmore College, where he later headed the English Department.

The deaths of both John and Sarah Rushmore during these years made it harder for their daughter to enter fully into local interests. Nevertheless, with the breaking up of her parents' home Jane's life became more surely oriented in Pennsylvania.

UNDER QUAKER APPOINTMENT

After she had been principal of Martin Academy for three years she tendered her resignation, which was reluctantly accepted by its Committee. She had worked hard and was worn with the exacting duties of an executive. At once Friends' Central School, then at Fifteenth and Race streets, Philadelphia, invited her to fill a vacancy in the boys' intermediate department. Here she would be situated where she could profit by the opportunities which a great city affords. She accepted the offer. Emma Wallace moved with her, going to the girls' intermediate department in the same school.

Jane's warm regard for Chester County Friends has never cooled, nor theirs for her. She has kept in close touch with a number of them and has often gone back to visit. When London Grove Meeting held a celebration of its two hundredth anniversary in 1914, she was in the great company that overflowed the large meeting house and filled the grounds outside. Later she wrote the foreword to the printed record of the occasion, saying,

> As we build our common everydays into the structure of an unchanging past, we are too close to the work to see it in true perspective, and each year's work shows little change in the completed whole. Only as the years are piled century-high can we justly estimate the influence which goes out from a Meeting like this upon community life. . . . The lesson of each worthy anniversary is pre-eminently that it is worth while to cultivate the same virtues and the same spirit in making our contribution to the work of this generation that, woven into the warp and woof of the history of two hundred years, makes the contemplation of the past a present satisfaction.

For those coming after, she said that the best wish she could make was that they might "absorb some degree of the moral vigor, social earnestness and spiritual power which for two centuries have radiated from this Meeting through the two branches of Friends."

CHAPTER IV

Social Pleasures and a Social Conscience

Friends' Central School provided Jane little scope for her kind of teaching. Pedagogy in the city schools was more formal in those days than the methods she had used in London Grove and Kennett. There was not much she could do about it from the position she was in, and she felt herself a misfit. After one year she resigned. Still tired from the hard work at Kennett, she decided to take a year's rest. Since she was living in Philadelphia with Emma Wallace, who continued at Friends' Central, Jane went back to take classes from time to time. But she was ready to stop teaching.

Meanwhile, a few years earlier, a new enterprise of Friendly connection had caught her attention. Her association with it, unofficial but close, was to last fifty years, and through it she was to meet socially many persons important in her later professional career. The undertaking began when Howard M. Jenkins, editor of the *Friends Intelligencer,* had listened to the earnest pleading of Samuel E. Griscom that a pleasant summer resort for Friends could be built on some undeveloped land which he owned in Monroe County, Pa. It was in the Pocono Mountains and there was a pretty trout stream running through it with a three-leap waterfall. Howard Jenkins and his son Charles persuaded Dr. William W. Speakman and Henry T. Paiste to join them and Samuel Griscom (all Race Street Yearly Meeting Friends) in incorporating the Buck Hill Falls Company and selling stock to more Philadelphia Quakers. It must be owned, however, that some of the conservative businessmen thought it a very doubtful investment and firmly refused it. In 1901 a small frame inn was opened. The same summer a few simple, rather crude cottages grouped themselves on adjacent lots, although all were substantial enough to keep within the stricture of the by-law which provided that no house costing less than $500 should be erected in the settlement. As a matter of fact the cost of the first one, including plumbing and painting, was almost $600.

Among the earliest cottagers was Susan P. Wharton, a niece of the Joseph Wharton who subsequently endowed the Wharton School of the University of Pennsylvania. Susan Wharton had enough faith in the new venture to believe that a sound use of some of her own rather slight resources might be to build two cottages for rent while she herself lived in a third. The founders were her friends. So were the three men who in 1902 joined the Board of Directors: S. Robinson Coale of Riverton, N. J.; Morgan Bunting of Lansdowne, Pa., the architect of the Inn and soon the secretary-treasurer of the Company; and Joseph S. Walton. All three were added to the Board after the tragic death in October of Howard Jenkins when he was carried over the Falls. Susan Wharton trusted the judgment of these men and shared their enthusiasm.

She was a woman fertile in creative ideas and of enormous energy. She launched herself wholeheartedly into the life of the settlement. She invited Jane Rushmore, whom she had known for years, to make the first of many visits to her cottage. The event proved to have a significant bearing on Jane's future field of usefulness, for while the two congenial spirits enjoyed vacation pleasures they often talked of plans for winter work. Summer activities were uppermost, however, at the beginning. One of Susan Wharton's early acts was to start a Nature Club which

SOCIAL PLEASURES AND A SOCIAL CONSCIENCE

grew and flourished over a considerable period. The hostess now managed to rouse in her guest an interest in ferns. Whatever Jane fixed her mind on she went into thoroughly, and soon she knew a great deal about these plants. One reason she liked them, she said, was because they grew in out-of-the-way places and climbing around to find them made entertaining excursions. The Nature Club had classes for adults, it organized bird walks, and especially it gave children happily occupied mornings during the years when "nature study" was a delightful new idea, as novel as having any organized amusement for children at a summer resort.

Before long Susan Wharton had produced some other fruitful proposals. She founded the Music Club to give opportunity for cultural expansion. Many Friends did not know much about music; vacation time was a good occasion to learn more. Then, as she watched the rapidly growing community at Buck Hill becoming less simple and less Quakerly year by year, she conceived the plan of having a course of lectures every summer to study life from the Friends' standpoint. Thus in 1924 came into being the Foxhowe Association which has been ever since a popular and honored institution.

Many people have inquired about the name with which Susan Wharton endowed this enterprise. "Fox," naturally, was taken from the name of the founder of Quakerism, and "howe" is an old English word meaning, in place names, a small hill. No reference was intended to Matthew Arnold's home.

The lively-minded originator of this association felt that people should not just vegetate in summer but should have intellectual exercise, so the Foxhowe programs were arranged with two weekday lectures plus one on Sunday

evening. For the first two summers a succession of lecturers came, each for a week or ten days. Then in 1926 Alexander C. Purdy, a professor at Hartford Theological Seminary, a Friend, and one who had taken part in the earlier programs, was made the resident director, a position he has held ever since. His Bible class on one weekday morning has from the start been a regular feature; the other hours have been set up variously by him and the successive presidents of the association.

During these years Jane Rushmore took part often as discussion leader and several times as a lecturer at the morning gatherings in the East Room, speaking on such subjects as education, democracy, the necessity for keeping sane (during the war years), and most recently on how modern poets look at life. Dr. Purdy has remarked of her lectures: "Her remarkable clarity and economy of speech and the sanity yet fearlessness of her thought together with a gift for concrete as against abstract expression made her words memorable."

Among the lecturers of the first two summers was the head of the Department of Biblical Literature at Earlham College, a Friends' minister named Clarence E. Pickett. In 1926 he and his wife were made host and hostess of the International House at Buck Hill, a cottage built by Marie C. Jenkins for foreign guests and so used for a number of years. Clarence and Lilly Pickett returned each summer through 1929. Their presence at Buck Hill brought them for the first time to the attention of eastern Friends, especially some who were looking for a new secretary for the American Friends Service Committee. The introduction proved to be one of notable importance.

Even before the Foxhowe Association had made its religious contribution to the settlement, there was already

SOCIAL PLEASURES AND A SOCIAL CONSCIENCE

established the regular Sunday meeting for worship. From the first Sunday the Inn was open to the present, without interruption, a short Friends' meeting has been held. In the first years everyone attended, including all the employees, both colored and white. The meeting has no status in any official body; it is entirely under the charge of the Board of Directors of the Company. Held in the largest room in the Inn, it has continued for fifty years to be one of the most sought out events at Buck Hill, at the height of the season often not only filling all available chairs and window ledges, but having a fair number of standees. For many guests it is their introduction to the Quaker way of worship. In a row of arm chairs facing the room sit such members of the Board as are in residence and a few other invited persons.

On occasions when Charles Jenkins found Jane Rushmore arriving for the service he usually asked her to join the group at the front. Often Jane demurred. "I direct thee to sit right there in the chair next to mine," said the not-to-be-denied man, and Jane complied. Whether in that chair or any other she often helped to present to the gathering in an acceptable way the basic Quaker message.

For years the most regular of these figures heading the meeting has been Charles N. Thompson, who came in 1907 to be general manager of the settlement and is now a director in the Company. As a boy growing up in Chester County he started working in Robert L. Pyle's store, where he was well known to Jane Rushmore and to all the local Friends. Some of them probably suggested him to the George School Committee, for when he was barely twenty-one years old he was appointed treasurer, bookkeeper, and purchasing agent for that school. During the eight years he was there he met emergencies with abounding resources and energy, whether the occasion was the cutting off of all the lights by the Newtown Power Company or the abrupt departure of the cook. More than once he wore the chef's cap and fed the school. He thus already knew S. Robinson Coale, a member of the school committee, when the Buck Hill Falls Company was looking for a successor to Robert Benson. Others of his George School friends he found in the summer colony at Buck Hill. In the succeeding years he has had a large share in its development into the immensely successful resort it now is. Exhibiting great imagination and vigor in carrying out new plans, he has at the same time been sensitive to the preservation of the simple, friendly, courteous atmosphere that has somehow remained personal in spite of the ever increasing size of the settlement.

In the more intimate days of its beginnings, one of the unique features of the Buck Hill summer was the Fourth of July celebration. The day began with a flag-raising at 9 A.M. Then the young people went into competitive rounds of sports while the children were herded down to a meadow by a small lake, where they indulged in firecrackers and noise to their hearts' content. At that time no one had dreamed of depriving children of firecrackers, and a noiseless Fourth would have been generally considered as defrauding the day of its proper honor. But this hotel was set in woodland where forest fires were an ever-present menace. For the safety of the settlement a new scheme had to be invented to satisfy the children. Here, then, was inaugurated probably the first, certainly one of the earliest, practices of a safe and sane Fourth. The older guests at the Inn were undisturbed, the children were happy in their remote and supervised racket, and everyone liked the innovation.

SOCIAL PLEASURES AND A SOCIAL CONSCIENCE

At dusk, with all the guests assembled in front of the Inn, Charles Jenkins gave out the awards to winners of the sports events, sometimes with a prize like a brass baggage check, and a rhyme. The day ended with a lantern parade. Since there was no electricity, every cottager had a supply of candle or oil lanterns. On the Fourth the householders were ranged at the Inn by order of the building of their cottages, and they marched along the paths making a charming sight from the porches as the lights flickered among the trees. Later, after the auditorium was built, the evening exercises always included the "Roll Call of the Signers." Himself an expert on the signers of the Declaration of Independence, Charles Jenkins offered a genuine autograph of a signer to any child under twelve who could recite all their names correctly. No matter how many children turned up to rattle off the list, he continued his gifts as long as he lived. If by any infrequent chance he was absent, his place as master of ceremonies was taken by Dr. William W. Speakman, whose gift for jokes and wisecracks made any event that he managed uproarious fun.

As Jane Rushmore watched the inexhaustible flow of ideas Charles Jenkins produced or promoted for the entertainment of guests in the early years of Buck Hill, she found herself becoming better and better acquainted with the man who was a rising leader in the Society of Friends and with whom she was later to have active association in the affairs of the Yearly Meeting.

In 1902 he had followed his father as president of the Buck Hill Falls Company. For forty-nine years thereafter the good judgment, financial ability, and steady hand of Charles F. Jenkins were the chief guide and reliance of the rapidly growing business. This remarkable man had a range of activity that few equal. His successful business was the publication of the *Farm Journal,* which became a leading farm paper in the United States. But this profession could not possibly contain the measure of his creative energy. Some of his vitality was absorbed by his Friendly connections. He was, for instance, clerk of Green Street Monthly Meeting for forty-two years, the first treasurer of the American Friends Service Committee, for forty years a member of the editorial board of the *Friends Intelligencer.* Devotion to early American history and to historic Germantown brought him into active participation in the Friends Historical Association, the Germantown Historical Society, and the Historical Society of Pennsylvania—of all of which he was at different times president—and stimulated his writing of several books on historical subjects. Although he had not had the opportunity to attend college himself, Swarthmore made him first a member and then president of its Board of Managers and granted him honorary membership in Phi Beta Kappa and an honorary Master's degree, to which honors were added Doctor of Laws degrees from Haverford and the University of Pennsylvania. The boards on which he served as a director, from the Provident Trust Company and important civic activities to obscure charities, all receiving alike his alert attention, are too numerous to list. At his home he established a horticulturally important hemlock arboretum where all nine species of hemlocks are growing as well as many varieties of other trees. His efforts were largely responsible for the adoption of the hemlock as the state tree of Pennsylvania. His death in July 1951 stilled a dynamo that had provided power for almost innumerable enterprises. In August of the same year a long-planned ceremony took place at Buck Hill Falls. The Company dedicated as "Jenkins Woods" a fine remnant of primeval forest standing on the north slope of Buck Hill between the Inn and the Falls, a beautiful and fitting memorial to Howard M. Jenkins and his son, Charles F. Jenkins.

Of all the younger man's interests, Buck Hill was probably nearest his heart. He took his able share in directing not only the fundamental social and financial policies of the Company but those which would forward Friendly interests. An example of the last was the series of Labor Day sport competitions with Pocono Manor after that Quaker rival hotel was built in 1902 by a group of Arch Street Friends. Teams, made up of guests, traveled from one resort to the other, making the most of their skills. The high-spirited fun of these occasions certainly had some part in breaking down the bars between Hicksite and Orthodox clans, a matter that rested heavily on Charles Jenkins' conscience. Straight through from its simplest beginnings Buck Hill had in its president the most genial, cordial, open-hearted host any resort could ask for, one who liked people and wanted them to enjoy themselves and each other. During the first years at the close of Sunday meeting he would take a rustic staff, gather all the guests, Jane Rushmore at least once among them, and lead them on a walk to the Falls, pointing out fine hemlocks, telling stories about the neighborhood, and offering bits of nature lore on this delightful pre-prandial tour. Always his fertile brain was bringing out something new. A guest still remembers the evening when one of the Shetland ponies he was raising at the time was led onto the lawn near the Inn porch where it was auctioned off with lively bidding for the benefit of the current charity. As soon as the bidding stopped and the money was paid, the winner would say that the feed cost too much or give some other excuse and the animal was put up again for new bids. The guests had superb enjoyment of the show, the cause benefited, and whether the pony ever really changed hands is lost in the mists of time.

Children were welcomed and their safety was the first consideration. When automobiles first began to appear on the roads they were forbidden in the settlement. If a cottager must bring an invalid or heavy equipment to his home, a permit was obtained and a bellboy stood on the running board to insure caution. Charles Thompson recalls a board meeting in 1907 when half an hour was spent considering whether or not to enlarge the Inn's garage. It already accommodated two cars. Finally it was decided to double the capacity so that the matter would be settled permanently.

Most of the early leaders at Buck Hill Jane Rushmore soon met if she did not already know them. She shared in the active social visiting in the cottages and at the Inn, especially on Sundays between meeting and dinner. She went to the big annual receptions at the Jenkins home. She took part in the intellectual activities. People all through the settlement were quickly made acquainted.

It was one of Jane's long-time friends who suggested a plan for increasing the Quaker leaven in the community. Joseph S. Walton, well known among Friends as an educator and a director of the Buck Hill Falls Company, was a man of many ideas. He saw the Inn becoming too high in price for some of the Friends who originally enjoyed it. He proposed a new building, simply constructed and furnished, where much less expensive accommodation could be had. It was erected on the slope below the Inn and named Griscom Hall after the earlier owner of the property. Only Friends may own stock in the Association which built the Hall and many of them patronized it at once.

SOCIAL PLEASURES AND A SOCIAL CONSCIENCE

For all the guests, however, the living is moderate in cost while they have access to the advantages of the whole settlement. Jane Rushmore served briefly as one of Griscom Hall's directors. Among the supporters of the Foxhowe lectures, of the several clubs, and of the community enterprises, she found that patrons of this hostelry were conspicuously loyal.

An important piece of work in the early years was the laying out and actual building or improving of the first footpaths to the Falls and through the settlement. This was taken up as his special pursuit by Henry Gawthrop, who spent the whole season at his cottage and who became a director in 1904. He was out on the land almost the summer long. At the same time his wife devoted much of her time and frail strength to the Greenleaf Library, a pleasant room built of logs at the corner of the Inn, with a growing number of books to loan. The kind of interest evinced in such ways as this by many individuals subsequently found expression in the activities of the Lot and Cottage Owners Association which now embraces about all the enterprises conducted at Buck Hill.

Jane's hostess of numerous vacations, Susan Wharton, as a stockholder and as a summer resident, followed every development at Buck Hill with intense interest. Her photograph hangs in the Greenleaf Library along with those of the early directors. With great satisfaction she saw that the growth of the Inn made the settlement a valued asset in the countryside. The building of cottages and the services required by the Inn soon gave year-round employment to many whose living had been rather cramped before. The Barrett Township Fair on Buck Hill grounds became an event important to both guests and permanent residents. The Barrett Friendly Library, a public library at the nearby village of Mountain Home, was built with Fair money aided by the contributed labor of local artisans. Charles Jenkins' Ayreshire cattle greatly improved the stock of the farmers in the county. Between the Inn and the township there is a coöperative arrangement whereby the Barrett Volunteer Fire Company stores its equipment on the Inn property and those who man it are drawn from both sources. With all these improving relationships Susan Wharton was in great sympathy, for she was a Friend with a social conscience that reached out to her community.

Another well-known figure of Buck Hill's first decade and a half, also touched by a social conscience, was that of Martha Schofield, one of the courageous women from the northern states who at the close of the Civil War had gone into the South to bring some opportunity for education to the Negroes. Undismayed by immense difficulties, she had succeeded in building up at Aiken, S. C., a large day and boarding school which has put hundreds, indeed by now thousands, of trained young people into good vocations. When one of the graduates of Schofield School became the first colored woman doctor in the country there was rejoicing. Martha Schofield's friends were legion throughout her adopted community, which she served for fifty years. A birthright member of Race Street Yearly Meeting, she found her summers at Buck Hill refreshing and congenial. There she was able to present the needs of her enterprise so successfully that for many years, and even for some time after her death in 1916, the proceeds of an annual Buck Hill Fair (not the later Barrett Township Fair) were entirely devoted to her work in South Carolina. Older than Susan Wharton, Martha Schofield preceded her in original work for the underprivileged, to whose need both women devoted most of their lives.

SOCIAL PLEASURES AND A SOCIAL CONSCIENCE

Great as was Susan Wharton's interest in all that made the surroundings of her summer home, her winter occupation was the center of her life and of her social concern in her most active years. Some time before Jane Rushmore came to Philadelphia this friend of hers had seen the condition of many South Philadelphia families and decided she must do something about it. So she had started what she called Starr Center at Sixth and Lombard streets, primarily for the distribution of coal and milk. She used to say, "I haven't a philanthropic bone in my body, but these people are being cheated." She meant that the poor who could buy coal only by the bucket were being charged an exorbitant price instead of being able to procure it in the most economical way. She put into operation a scheme of purchasing coal at the mines, persuading dealers to store it at a small price, and then selling it by the quarter- or half-ton on orders sent in by the Center to families who accumulated the price by penny savings. In somewhat the same way milk for babies was obtained from the Modified Milk Society and sold to mothers. The families collected their money for these expenses by stamp books issued by a small neighborhood penny-savings bank started by Theodore Starr and bearing his name. The bank gave out the cards or books; the stamps to go on them were sold by the visitors from Starr Center, which also took its name from the bank's founder. The Center in addition operated a library and a kindergarten, its only free services.

When Jane Rushmore was visiting her friend Susan Wharton at Buck Hill in the summer of 1905, the latter explained her need of a new executive secretary for the Center and asked Jane if she would take the job. Jane thought she might like to, but said she must look into it in her own way first. So she returned to Philadelphia to visit the scene, announcing to the staff merely that she might be interested in working there. She went through each department, asking the various staff members to explain just how their different branches worked and accompanying the visitors for several days on their rounds. After a thorough examination she was ready to accept the position, though doubtful of success in a field for which she had received no special training.

Susan Wharton was herself at Starr Center almost every day. She lived further uptown, on Clinton Street, and Mary Richmond, then general director of the Associated Charities of Philadelphia, lived with her. Miss Richmond's advice was very much valued; the two women talked over the problems of Starr Center together, though Susan Wharton had no need of being pushed along by anyone else. She had an enormous store of energy and vigor. She would, as her cousin-in-law, Dr. Walter Mendelson, said of her, unhesitatingly attempt the impossible and somehow succeed.

She would have accomplished even more than she did if she had had some business training. Jane found almost her first task to be that of bringing order into the business transactions. She spent many hours going over the coal and milk accounts, which were tedious and trying but were the core of the enterprise. After a time the office of treasurer was assumed by Thomas S. Gates, later president of the University of Pennsylvania. Every month he went carefully over the previous month's expenditures and the balances in the bank, and then drew a check for the projected payments of the next month. Jane had prepared the figures and went over them with him, gaining business experience that was to be very valuable to her later.

An excellent board of trustees had been built up, chaired

SOCIAL PLEASURES AND A SOCIAL CONSCIENCE

by Charles E. Pancoast, president of the Guarantee Trust Company. From him as well as from Thomas Gates the executive secretary learned a good deal about investments. She was impressed, too, with the way Mr. Pancoast conducted the board meetings. There were no Friends on the board except herself, Susan Wharton, and Esther Morton Smith, yet as each subject came up it was thoroughly discussed all around the table, everyone was consulted, and when the board was pretty much a unit in its decision the president would call for a motion almost as a Friends' clerk would frame a minute of the sense of the meeting. The minutes were kept by Jane, so she was very much aware of the procedure. All the board appreciated Susan Wharton's vision and her habit of thinking things through. They supported her well.

To finance the work of the Center, Susan Wharton had developed a long subscription list. While the basic principle of the settlement was to have the neighbors save to pay for what they received and so form habits of thrift, of course they did not actually pay the full cost of the services, which had to be met by donations. A clerk was installed who made lists and kept files of contributors. Jane took over the writing of the appeal letters. She was interested to observe that it was often the fifth letter to the same person that brought the response. There were some large donors whose gifts made possible certain specific projects. Such a giver was Dr. George Woodward of Chestnut Hill, who had built a model tenement nearby, the Casa Novello. He established a milk station on its first floor which was operated by the Starr Center but financed entirely by Dr. Woodward.

Jane soon discovered that the milk distribution was not sufficiently regulated. Mothers had been buying the modified milk according to their own ideas of their babies' need and their own ability to pay. Jane suggested having a doctor come to put matters on a better basis. Dr. William W. Cadbury, afterward a Friends' missionary to China, served in this way for about three years, examining the mothers and babies, prescribing the formulas and the hours of feeding. The mothers were not allowed to buy the milk until they had had this examination. Since most of the women could not compass a time schedule without help, each was given a picture of a clock with bottles hung on the proper hours for feeding.

Visitors, carefully supervised, called at local homes, sold savings stamps, listened to family troubles, and sometimes gave advice. Some two to three hundred people belonged to the Coal Club. There were also a good number in the Rainy Day Society, whose emblem was the picture of an umbrella on the card, and whose savings were to provide doctor's fees and medicine in case of illness. At the end of the year if the money had not been used for sickness it was repaid to the member.

It did not need long acquaintance with the district for Susan Wharton to discover that many school children had no breakfast. Thereupon she devised a plan of cheap lunches sold at a few schools. This was really the beginning of penny lunches in the city of Philadelphia. When Jane looked into this department she saw that the food being sold to the children was not very sensible, so she found a dietitian just graduated from Drexel Institute who thereafter made out the orders for what should be offered. Willing to come without salary for the experience, this young woman, Alice Boughton, subsequently organized the school lunch system for the public schools of Philadelphia. Mr. Henry H. Bonnell, a member of the Center's

SOCIAL PLEASURES AND A SOCIAL CONSCIENCE

board who took special interest in this project, made a large contribution to the salary of the lunch dispenser. Another prominent Philadelphian who served on the board and took an active part in all that went on was S. Rowland Morgan, a man of much graciousness of manner and one genuinely devoted to the service of those with few advantages or in distress.

Jane insists that all the ideas for this day settlement were Susan Wharton's. But it was Jane who made the ideas work, who supplied continuity, and who kept the financial base sound. It was excellent training in organization as well, for by the end of her service of six years there were seventeen workers on the staff. At that time Susan Wharton had become less active, and Jane was being pressed to accept another position.

The years of living in Philadelphia while she taught at Friends' Central and worked at Starr Center gave to Jane Rushmore and also to Emma Wallace an opportunity to indulge their insatiable thirst for knowledge. A large city provided opportunities not available before. For instance, they enrolled at the Wagner Institute for courses in electricity and sound. They found most of their fellow students to be in the electrical trades, and while the class was large, very few of them, and no other women, turned up for the examination at the end of the course. More conventional than courses in electricity were those on Saturday mornings at the University of Pennsylvania, where Jane studied mathematics and Latin while Emma Wallace took German.

Before this, while she was still teaching, Jane had already enjoyed various summer schools, one operated at Huntingdon, Pa., by Joseph Walton and Martin Brumbaugh, and another at the Oswego, N. Y., School of Languages under Dr. Sauveur. At the latter Jane devoted herself to German in one of the very early experiments with the natural method. Only German was spoken and heard in class, in the boardinghouse, and in chapel. The students went to five classes every day, with a different man teaching each hour. This course had made it possible for Jane to prepare her own pupils for college entrance examinations in German. Wherever she was, Jane always found the sources of intellectual stimulus. Her alert mind seized upon every new field that came within her range.

She had lived the first half of her life adding to her knowledge, her training, her acquaintance, her experience. She had been an outstanding teacher in Chester County and a competent executive in Philadelphia. She was already marked as a woman of unusual ability. But she had not stretched her capacities to their fullest extent, nor had she found the area in which she could function at the top of her powers. She was not consciously seeking an opportunity to make the best use of the tempered instrument her mind had become. When the opening appeared, she did not immediately recognize it in the proposal that she become secretary of the new Friends Central Bureau. She was favorably inclined toward it, however, because of a long experience, going back more than fifteen years, as a voluntary partner in another experiment begun by her religious society. This experiment had by 1900 developed into the Friends General Conference.

CHAPTER V

Seven Yearly Meetings at Work Together

Friends did not begin to stir into new manifestations of life for a generation after the numbing effect of the 1827 Separation. The need which then galvanized the Hicksite group into motion was that of religious instruction for their children. Here and there an attempt was made to start a First-day school. Sometimes it was the isolated effort of a single person who felt that in a religious society where definite instruction was not a part of the form of worship, children should have something to replace the formerly more common family religious meetings and family Bible readings. The impetus once given, the development of classes and organization began to spread.

In a number of places the old feeling persisted that First-day schools were "creaturely activity," God alone being able to give understanding of the Scripture. One by one, however, the various Yearly Meetings granted official recognition of the new institution. Race Street Yearly Meeting, the last to do so, withheld until 1884 its formal approval, although First-day schools had been appearing in its bailiwick ever since the first three had been set up. These were at Reading, Pa., in 1859, at Germantown in 1860, neither of which was continuous, and then at Green Street, Philadelphia, in 1861. First-day school unions also grew up, each embracing the schools of a fairly wide area, usually that of the Quarterly Meeting. These unions soon became established within Race Street boundaries also.

In 1867 Eli M. Lamb, principal of Baltimore Friends School, was the leading spirit in bringing together a number of Friends at West Chester, Pa., to consider methods of improving religious teaching. As a result, a general First-day School Conference was held in Philadelphia the following year. Unions of all the seven Hicksite Yearly Meetings were represented. That conference was fruitful enough for its promoters to institute regular annual gatherings which met almost without a break until 1882, when they entered a new phase. Eli Lamb's idea was actually the small spring whose increasing waters were to become more than thirty years later the full-flowing river of Friends General Conference.

Vigor was given to the young movement by the great need for lesson helps. Although lessons put out by other denominations were often used, it was soon discovered that inexperienced volunteer teachers needed printed material written especially for Friends. The fact that the early First-day School Conferences had a specific function in producing this matter gave them stability from the start.

By the end of the seventies another concern was growing up, especially in Illinois Yearly Meeting under the leadership of Jonathan W. Plummer. This Chicago merchant was an active Friend who had helped to create Illinois Yearly Meeting in 1875.* Because Hicksite Friends were not evangelistic the great wave of interest in foreign missionary enterprise had by-passed them, but, to a certain degree taking its place, there developed a strong conscience about social conditions in local communities. Sometimes local associations were set up outside the direct jurisdiction of the Society of Friends, though composed largely of its members; sometimes committees were formed under a Monthly Meeting. When the latter

---

* Cf. Albert T. Mills, "Jonathan W. Plummer," in *Quaker Torchbearers* (Philadelphia, 1943), pp. 174 ff.

course was taken the group assumed the formidable name of Committee on Philanthropic Labor, and the activities were various. Some committees only appropriated money to civic undertakings, but more often special work in prisons, settlements, for Indians, temperance, and other causes was taken up. Jonathan Plummer was one of those particularly uneasy at the national government's treatment of American Indians, at the lack of training facilities for Negroes, and at the denial of voting and other rights to women. After the First-day School Conference of 1868 he began thinking of a more comprehensive gathering to cover the social concerns of Friends. Largely because of his persuasion Illinois Yearly Meeting in 1878 sent an epistle to the other Hicksite groups proposing such a general conference.

Action was not precipitous. But in 1881 representatives of three of the Yearly Meetings—Baltimore, Ohio, and Illinois—came together in Salem, Ohio, to organize the Friends Union for Philanthropic Labor. It met in Waynesville, Ohio, the next year, immediately following the First-day School Conference. All local Monthly Meetings were asked to send in regular reports to this and subsequent conferences. Of course some localities were much more active than others, but the existence of the Union and the necessity for making reports proved an impetus for further work.

Because many attenders were interested in both religious education and philanthropy it became the practice to hold the two gatherings at the same place, one following directly after the other. The idea of holding these conferences only biennially also gained favor, and with some exceptions the pattern of meeting together every other year became fixed. In the eighties the total group was of such moderate size that the visitors could be entertained in the homes of resident Friends. By 1892, however, the numbers had increased so that the homes in Lincoln, Va., the chosen meeting place, were severely taxed and a change of plan had to be made, especially since further developments were under way.

When the Columbia Exposition opened in Chicago in 1893, great stimulus was given to some groups not directly connected with the World's Fair but having international ties. Among them was a World Parliament of Religions, to which Howard M. Jenkins was appointed to represent Race Street Yearly Meeting. He found himself in a large group from the United States and Canada at the sessions assigned to Quakers. Jonathan Plummer, chairman of the Hicksite section, gave an important address. This early effort to bring the various denominations into some sort of working partnership was an inspiration to Howard Jenkins, who came home full of the idea that at least the seven Hicksite Yearly Meetings could get together at once. He began active promotion of a general religious conference for all the Yearly Meetings to be held in 1894 at the same time as the older two. Contemporaneously Edward H. Magill, then retired from the presidency of Swarthmore College, was urging a conference on education as a concern in which Friends had been most active from the beginning of their history. With the prospect of convening at one place four relatively independent groups (on First-day schools, philanthropy, religion, and education) the planners obviously had to find a location with plenty of space. A large Friends' boarding school was chosen at Chappaqua, N. Y., for the 1894 summer convocation.

Friends arrived from the seven Yearly Meetings: Illinois, Indiana, and Ohio on the west; Genesee on the north; New York, Philadelphia, and Baltimore on the east. They overflowed the accommodations in the school building although cots had been lined up, dormitory fashion, in the attic. Tents were set up on the campus. Guests allotted to them found they made for pretty primitive living, with water leaking through when it rained and only a rope strung down the middle to hang clothes on. Among those so berthed was Jane Rushmore, who was making her first appearance at these occasions. She was a representative to the First-day School Conference from New York.

The program was just to all the interests which had set it up. There were four addresses of welcome, four chairmen, and at the end four adjournments. Jane, as one of the younger members, often took a seat in the rear of the auditorium where it was sometimes difficult to hear. Edward Magill, already deaf, always sat on the platform bringing with him his long black metal ear trumpet. Jane soon observed that when Edward Magill laid his trumpet on his lap nothing of importance was being said and she relaxed.

The Young Friends Association of Philadelphia had also in 1894 issued a call for an informal conference of young people at Chappaqua to arrange for organizing this group, and a large number were present. At their first meeting for worship all the time was taken up by older Friends who seemed to enjoy speaking to a large audience of young persons. Jane was a prime mover in arranging for a second meeting. Preparatory to it William M. Jackson, the presider, at the request of the young Friends announced that the presence of older Friends, and their silent participation, would be welcome. One of those admonished asked, "Aren't you going to have any preaching?" and was confuted when Jane replied, "Oh, I didn't know Friends arranged for that. Do they?"

Two years later Swarthmore College was selected as the site for the four interests meeting together. This was the last time that free entertainment of visitors was undertaken. Philadelphia Friends raised $10,000 by subscription to meet the expenses, but such a cost was too great to undertake as a recurrent burden. From then on attenders paid their own way.

The Swarthmore group of conferences in 1896 was the largest that had been held to date, because of the active work of several leaders. Jonathan W. Plummer had found very able collaboration for the many forms of philanthropic pursuits. From New York came John W. Hutchinson, a leader on parole and other legal aspects of imprisonment, and Anna M. Jackson who poured out energy in behalf of the colored people. Dr. O. Edward Janney of Baltimore was a valiant crusader for "social purity," taking over the mantle of that then almost unmentionable cause from Aaron M. Powell. The recording secretary of this Conference was Sarah W. Matthews, also of Baltimore.

William W. Birdsall, a rising educator in Philadelphia, joined Edward H. Magill in the new program of the Education Conference. William Birdsall, principal of the Boys' Department of Friends' Central School and later president of Swarthmore College, like Edward Magill had a Quakerly as well as a professional concern for education. Joseph A. Bogardus of New York, Eli M. Lamb of Baltimore, Edward Coale of Illinois, and Robert M. Janney of Philadelphia, all of them prominent in their own Meetings, took a large part in the consideration of religious teaching.

SEVEN YEARLY MEETINGS AT WORK TOGETHER

Among the attenders at Swarthmore was one whose presence was to have long consequences. John William Graham of England made in 1896 the first of his several trips to visit American Friends. It was almost unheard of for a Hicksite gathering to have a visit from an English Quaker. John William Graham intended to approach with an open mind all Quaker groups in the United States, hoping to bring the branches closer together. He felt that London, as the parent Yearly Meeting, had a responsibility to use its influence to heal the schisms that perhaps might not have taken place if English leaders had been more alert. He had, however, no official support and came entirely under his own conscience. The Religious Conference was glad when he agreed to give two addresses, one on the Adult School movement conducted by English Friends, and one on a purely religious topic. Unfortunately he was on the whole disappointed on this visit to find many Hicksites not very well educated, and as he traveled in the West he was discouraged at the procedures of the Friends' churches. Nevertheless he returned to this country on a number of subsequent occasions and became a most sympathetic counselor to the Friends of the liberal branch, as doubtless to other groups, making the sense of kinship with London increasingly alive.

The Conference of 1898 at Richmond, Ind., smaller than the previous one, made abundantly clear to everyone that the structure of four separate unions was extremely cumbersome. Plans were set up to unite the assembly at its next gathering, and in 1900, at Chautauqua, N. Y., the groups met as a single body. Jonathan Plummer when he first founded the Union on Philanthropic Labor had advocated a general conference; now it had come about. In the new body the Religious Conference was given up as a separate section since the combining unions were all felt to be varying expressions of the religious concern which was the essential emphasis of the whole undertaking. Thus the three divisions of First-day School, Philanthropic Labor, and Education became the constituent parts of the new Friends General Conference. Its formation preceded by two years the establishment of the Five Years Meeting, representing most of the Orthodox Yearly Meetings in America.

Friends General Conference was not planned to be, and never has been, a supra-Meeting. It has no authority over Yearly Meetings. Its function is mutual help, encouragement, and understanding. Its general organizing unit is the Central Committee of One Hundred, appointed in fractions proportionate to their size by all the Yearly Meetings except, in the beginning, Philadelphia, whose representatives were unofficial until 1912. Members of the Central Committee now sit almost daily during the biennial Conference, meet for a week in September in the alternating years, and have other less regular sessions. The Committee actively directs the setting up of the biennial meetings, appointing the several subcommittees for program, for arrangements with the host city and its hotels, for recreation, and all the other necessities involved in taking care of a large number of people for a week. The publication of First-day school lessons and other religious education material is supervised by the Central Committee, which of course also controls the budget and financing of the whole Conference.

Two years before the formation of the united Conference there had appeared at Richmond in 1898 a new face, and a new voice had surprised and stirred the gathering. They belonged to Henry W. Wilbur, a member of New

York Yearly Meeting who had been a small-town newspaper editor and printer. He was a liberal of intense convictions. He came to Chautauqua sure that the new united Conference had great possibilities. Even it, however, would not alone be enough to hold off a slow death for the now diminishing Yearly Meetings. The Society of Friends, he believed, had an unfulfilled mission to many for whom its simple faith would be a healing and strengthening experience. But Friends had an aversion to proselyting and had little skill interpreting their religious ideas to others. He was on fire to remedy this state of affairs. Under his stimulation a new Committee for the Advancement of Friends' Principles was added as a working unit by the Conference of 1900 with Henry Wilbur as chairman.

Jane Rushmore was also beginning to rise into prominence in the affairs of the Conference. Very early she started her long list of services to it. In turn she took part in the Philanthropic, First-day School, and Education Committees, the Advancement Committee, and was many times a member of the Central Committee. She began in 1898 as secretary of the Philanthropic. Here she saw the reports sent in by Yearly Meeting Unions on their diverse social efforts. The number of subjects was long, for many years including proper publications, temperance, child welfare, tobacco and other narcotics, Indian affairs, colored people, gambling, prison reform, capital punishment, peace, and social purity. Temperance was one of the most vigorous and widespread of the early activities, closely followed by work among Indians, for which individual Meetings supported a number of agents who worked in the reservations. Augustus Brosius of Pennsylvania was one of the well-known men in this field. Belief that criminals could and should be rehabilitated was part of Quaker principle, and it took several forms in the various Meetings—having police matrons put in jails where women offenders were held, working for parole, and seeking to reduce vengeful punishments. Peace between nations has never ceased to be one of the most ardently pursued efforts through all the years when interest in other topics rose and fell in slow undulations.

In recent years the philanthropic concerns have been arranged in three groups: Economic Problems, Peace and World Understanding, and Social Order. These, together with Education, Religious Education, and Advancement, constitute the present six standing committees of Friends General Conference. The Committee on Economic Problems, appointed in 1940, has published a monthly or bimonthly *Newsletter* to sharpen the awareness of Friends to the connection between religion and economic factors in the world. Work for peace has had a greatly enlarged place since the first World War. Following several devoted leaders, Esther Holmes Jones, now chairman of the Peace Committee, is an accredited observer at the Social and Economic Council of the United Nations, representing the General Conference; she guides an unceasing stream of Friends and others to see the workings of that international body; she does a great deal of speaking on it before both Friends and outside groups. The Committee is a member of the National Peace Conference and is represented on the Friends Committee on National Legislation. It sends information to local Meetings on peace issues and it arranges the biennial Conference program on this subject.

After a few years in the philanthropic work of the Conference, Jane Rushmore moved into the First-day school field. Over the whole half-century of Conference history, the First-day School Committee, now called the Religious Education Committee, has been exceedingly active. It has kept up continuous publication. As early as 1885 it had started to print and distribute First-day school lesson leaves, which by 1904 advanced to a regular graded series published quarterly and still continued, though in more modern form. By 1908 Jane was named general secretary of the Conference First-day School Committee, an unpaid officer giving in her free time counseling to the schools. Very soon she saw the need for the Conference to reach the teachers with further assistance than the graded lessons. After the Friends Central Bureau began functioning she suggested that, with the facilities of the Bureau, a quarterly *First-day School Bulletin* be printed and circulated to all First-day school teachers in the Conference. Publication began in 1916. Later called the *Religious Education Bulletin,* it has appeared regularly ever since, with a circulation in 1952 of 1400.

As the singing of hymns in First-day schools became more common, Jane proposed printing a small hymnal wherein the words would agree with the teaching of Friends and the music be dignified and beautiful. The idea was quickly approved, but there was no money. At the close of the committee session where the matter had been discussed, William C. Biddle of Lansdowne, Pa., came to Jane and asked how much such a book would cost. "I don't know," she said, "but perhaps a small volume of about thirty hymns, with music, might cost in the neighborhood of $800." William Biddle turned and brought Edward Cornell of New York and Robert Roberts of Baltimore into the conversation. In a few minutes these three men had agreed to loan the necessary money. Jane lost no time. The first little paper-bound book appeared in November 1919. The edition sold out in three months with the borrowed money paid back and enough left over for the second edition. Each edition since has been paid for by the proceeds of the previous one and has cost the Conference nothing.

Feeling that printed material alone was not sufficient help for First-day school teachers, Bliss Forbush of Baltimore wanted to promote definite leadership training in the Society of Friends for all work in religious education. For this purpose he designed a correspondence course, asking Jane Rushmore's help. The first year there was a great response. Bliss Forbush took charge of the course on the Bible, and Jane of the one on the Society of Friends. She read and corrected about a thousand papers, an unexpected burden added to her regular tasks. After some time, when enthusiasm for correspondence courses died down, Bliss Forbush developed leadership training institutes which were held at Camp Keewadin, near Annapolis, Md., and later at Pendle Hill, the Friends' adult school at Wallingford, Pa. When he no longer had time to carry so much responsibility for the institutes they were given up, but other activities at Pendle Hill have to a large extent taken their place.

Still another enterprise of religious education under the aegis of the Conference was a series of summer schools. The first one of these, the idea of Joseph S. Walton and Jesse H. Holmes, took place in 1903 at Buck Hill Falls. Buck Hill had opened only two years before. Many Friends were eager to see it, the Inn made special rates for food, cottagers offered rooms. Forty to fifty persons attended and were given an excellent program for a week. At a second "First-day School Assembly" at Buck Hill in 1905 George A. Barton of Bryn Mawr College and William Wallace Fenn of Harvard lectured, Jesse Holmes led classes on social concerns, and Joseph Walton on Friends' books and journals. For recreation the Buck Hill residents wanted to show off the beautiful country to these visitors, so three-seater buckboards were filled and driven through the woods to Canadensis, down the Broadhead Creek and back by way of Mountain Home. Members of the summer school were asked to make up their own carriage loads. Jane Rushmore chose to take some older Friends who seemed to be alone. They proved to be the most interesting group of riders, for among them were those acquainted with trees, plants, rocks, and other nature lore. The excursion of perhaps ten miles was a success.

After the experiments at Buck Hill, summer schools were continued under the leadership of Henry Wilbur and the Advancement Committee, alternating every two years with the biennial Conferences. Pennsylvania meeting places were selected: George School, West Chester, and Swarthmore. At Swarthmore, bicycles were brought by a number of young people, who one day began baiting Isaac Wilson, a prominent minister from Bloomfield, Ontario, and Jane Rushmore to have a race around the campus. When each demurred on the ground of having no "wheel," machines were gladly offered, on the assumption that neither contestant knew how to ride. To the surprise and slight anxiety of the owners two were accepted; the elderly gentleman and the not yet middle-aged lady mounted with assurance and dashed off in great style. While Isaac Wilson won the race, both were received back with acclaim. The bicycles were intact.

A few summer schools were held in the Midwest as an extension of the series. At one of them, in Benjaminville, Ill., Jane Rushmore discussed work for Friends in the country neighborhoods. She had gone to Illinois Yearly Meeting in McNabb several days previously, hoping to get some points for her talks. She found that the material gathered at home was so irrelevant to the needs of Illinois communities that she was obliged to abandon her carefully prepared notes and begin where Illinois requirements were most evident. There were a number of fine intelligent Friends in the Illinois Meeting, of whom Elizabeth Coale of Benjaminville was one. The members as a whole did their best to preserve their heritage but made little impression on their neighborhoods. They needed help. In the summer school that Jane attended in 1913 she did her best to work out with them some advances.

Meanwhile Arch Street Yearly Meeting, almost unknown to Race Street, had since 1900 also been holding summer schools largely modeled on the school at Woodbrooke, England. A new chapter started for both groups when in 1923 a united summer school was held at Haverford under the auspices of Haverford College, the Extension Committee of Arch Street Yearly Meeting, the Advancement Committee of Friends General Conference, and Woolman School, another project initiated by Henry Wilbur. Similar united summer schools were held alternately at Haverford and Swarthmore until they were later absorbed in the summer term of Pendle Hill. The early conception of Joseph Walton and Jesse Holmes was significant because it was the first organized reaching-out of Hicksite Friends for systematic adult instruction in the Bible and social concerns.

Arranging summer school programs led Henry Wilbur's active mind to the possibility of further expansion. He was convinced that there should be some sort of year-round school for adult Friends in a religious society which had no professional leadership. His enthusiasm led his committee forward in the steps necessary for the establishment of an institution for "social and religious training" which would attempt to prepare rank and file Friends for better service in their meetings. His death prevented him from bringing the school into being, but Dr. O. Edward Janney, an ardent believer in it, pushed on. On January 4, 1915, Woolman School opened at Swarthmore, using a house near the campus bought by Emma C. Bancroft and loaned rent-free to the school. William I. and Hannah Clothier Hull were the resident host and hostess. With the help of faculty borrowed from the college, three courses were offered for three months each, and could be taken separately or in sequence for a full academic year.

Arranging the courses of study without a full-time director, as was first attempted, proved very difficult, although Bird T. Baldwin, then teaching at the college, did his best in his spare time as unpaid director. Before long a different method was acknowledged to be necessary. After considerable search Elbert Russell was in 1917 chosen for the post in spite of opposition by some Friends who thought it entirely unsuitable to appoint a Five Years Meeting member. He was willing to come only on the condition that members of both Philadelphia Yearly Meetings be on the board and that Friends of all branches be welcome at the school. This was agreed to and the choice of director proved a fortunate one. Elbert Russell's understanding of Hicksite views, his lovable disposition, his scholarly knowledge of the Bible and ability to interpret it in today's terms and language won for him the devoted friendship of the General Conference. In this early period Jane Rushmore served on the board of Woolman School and taught some classes during the enforced absence of the director. Elbert Russell in 1926 was called by the American Friends Service Committee for work in Europe and resigned from the school. Subsequently he went to Duke University where he was professor and then dean at the Divinity School. He was succeeded at Woolman School by Caroline G. Norment, a member of Baltimore Yearly Meeting.

Although modeled somewhat on what Friends in England were successfully doing at Woodbrooke, Woolman School was an ambitious undertaking so new to American Friends that it was hard to secure the attendance necessary to maintain it. After some vicissitudes, including a move from Swarthmore to Wyncote, Pa., in 1925, which came about after Mary Lippincott gave the school her house there and $10,000, the project had to be suspended and in 1929 the property was sold. Nevertheless, its existence had so opened the eyes of Friends to the possibilities of such a school that when a plan of reorganization was proposed later in 1929 the constituency was ready. A new school named Pendle Hill was set up at Wallingford, Pa., using the funds of Woolman School and having a board with a wide representation of General Conference, Arch Street, and Five Years Meeting Friends.

This board persuaded Dr. Henry T. Hodgkin to open the venture as its first director in 1930. An Englishman by birth, a medical missionary in China for many years, and a founder of the Fellowship of Reconciliation, he came with enthusiasm to this experiment. With each year the position of the institution has become firmer. John Hughes, then Richard Gregg, succeeded Henry Hodgkin. and were followed by the codirectors Howard H. and Anna Cox Brinton. Under this series of able leaders the school has given an uninterrupted service of high value for twenty years. Institutes for Meeting workers, training for Service Committee volunteers for overseas, weekend conferences, courses in religious and social studies throughout the year now make a busy campus. The school's recognized place among Friends is the fulfilment of Henry W. Wilbur's dream.

The various religious-training enterprises of Friends General Conference, which were begun merely with the printing of lesson series under the First-day School Committee, thus spread into teachers' institutes, summer schools, and Woolman School, and were in part carried by the Advancement Committee.

In the beginning the Advancement Committee did not have Henry Wilbur as its secretary. When it was set up in 1900 he was chairman and Jesse H. Holmes was the recording secretary. Both of these men had a good deal of drive and both believed ardently in the new venture. On February 1, 1905, Henry Wilbur was made full-time executive with an office in the Young Friends Association Building at 140 North Fifteenth Street, Philadelphia. At once he set to work on one of his main concerns which he developed into another major field of Conference activity, that of building up the local Meetings. The tearing wounds of the 1827 Separation had resulted in a withdrawal into its own community by the Hicksite branch, and a desire to keep its own inheritance pure. So ingrown had the Society become that it was most unusual for any outsider to ask to join it, and the belief was widely held in the non-Quaker world that no one could be a Friend unless he had been born one or had married one. Of course a steady decline in members resulted, which for many years entirely failed to impress the Yearly Meetings.

With the rise of Friends General Conference this problem was at last faced. A sense of united work in the various branches of philanthropy, the new aids for First-day school teaching, the stimulating effect of social acquaintance at the big conferences, all had their influence. In addition the Advancement Committee made a frontal attack on the situation. Henry Wilbur was a born orator. He began at once to travel throughout all the Yearly Meetings, rousing them to some sense of vitality and unity. It was uphill work to reverse a trend of seventy-five years' growth, but his infectious spirit gave the Meetings courage. He talked common sense and he stirred young people to action. Also he discovered where scattered Friends were living, put them in touch with each other, and suggested that they try to meet together. Slowly two or three new Meetings arose, new interest sprang up whose fruitage Henry Wilbur did not live to see. After an interval of several months following his death in 1914, J. Barnard Walton was appointed secretary of the Advancement Committee and later secretary of Friends General Conference. He has continued Henry Wilbur's plan of visiting widely among all the Meetings, has arranged for visits by other Friends, kept a file of nonresident members of various Meetings, corresponded with many seekers about the Quaker way of life, and conducted the executive work of the office.

Efforts were made early by the Conference to keep alive the Meetings in Iowa and eastern Ohio, but for them help came too late. Iowa Meetings slowly vanished. They were not a separate Yearly Meeting, but a part of Illinois, which was not strong enough to give support to these widely scattered small groups. Ohio was counted among the constituent Yearly Meetings when the General Conference was first established in 1900. After 1918 its

SEVEN YEARLY MEETINGS AT WORK TOGETHER

Yearly Meeting sessions were not held, but a Representative Committee still counted as part of the Conference. Three dwindling Meetings continued for a time and then ceased to function.

Thereafter, the Yearly Meeting participants in the General Conference were six: Illinois, Indiana, Genesee, New York, Philadelphia, and Baltimore. Philadelphia was able to extend its influence to the far West through the establishment of Orange Grove Monthly Meeting in Pasadena, Cal. Its first members had migrated from Philadelphia and wished to belong to Race Street Yearly Meeting. It therefore is an integral unit in the Conference. Recently Cambridge Monthly Meeting, a member of New England Yearly Meeting, became a part of the Conference as a United Meeting. Other new Meetings have been invited to join with the Conference and to participate in its activities.

Of the three Yearly Meetings that lie back of the eastern seaboard, Genesee was at the beginning small and weak. Nevertheless, it furnished at the turn of the century three outstanding Hicksite preachers: Sunderland P. Gardiner, who often visited New York Yearly Meeting; John J. Cornell, who later moved to Baltimore becoming quite a power there; and Isaac Wilson. Although he had very little education, Isaac Wilson became the fluent and vigorous preacher of a simple faith based on the life of Jesus. He sometimes appeared in the pulpit of the Bloomfield Methodist Church, but his service was most notable in the long distances he traveled under religious concern, visiting Friends' Meetings widely. His love of children, his interest in people and tolerance of their ways and opinions made him as welcome as he was constant in his attendance at the biennial General Conferences. He was active until about two years before he died in 1932 at the age of ninety-three.

The Zavitz family of Coldstream, long an important part of Genesee Yearly Meeting, have contributed much toward its growth. They had many members who became prominent professionally and were influential among Friends. Charles Zavitz was one of the founders of the Canadian Friends' Service Committee, whose activities are similar to those of the British and American counterparts.

In almost as precarious a situation as Genesee in the early years of the Conference were Indiana and Illinois, for the groups were small and distances between them great. Indiana was perhaps a little larger at the start. Centering in Richmond it was greatly outnumbered by the pastoral, evangelical Friends, but it developed some strong leaders. Among them was Frances M. Robinson. Another was Edith Winder, who studied at Woodbrooke and returned to a good many years of active work in Indiana where, among other things, she made a clear and discriminating survey of Indiana and Illinois Yearly Meetings. Later this fine and unassuming woman came to Woolman House to act as hostess. In that capacity she was able to do considerable visiting among eastern Friends until her marriage to William Littleboy and her departure for England.

Illinois, covering a wide territory, was definitely at first a rural Yearly Meeting, holding its annual sessions at Clear Creek Meeting, near McNabb. There was little business to transact and the sessions were informal. Clarence and Albert Mills, Charles Whitney and others were leading Friends downstate. Afterward a group formed in Chicago around Jonathan Plummer, Thomas

A. Jenkins, and, among others, the family of Clement and Louella Flitcraft. They received inspiration from Jane Addams and her co-workers at Hull House, although Jane Addams did not become a member, nor did most of her staff. The interest of this Monthly Meeting in philanthropic concerns and its close connection with the General Conference brought new life into the whole area. The Conference set up summer schools in both Indiana and Illinois with good lectures, discussions, and social features. The fine start made by Thomas Jenkins's daughter Beatrice in work among young people was unfortunately cut off by her early death.

Slowly the tide has turned. A renewed interest in Friends has been manifested by the public, stimulated not only by the Conference but by simultaneous encouragement from the American Friends Service Committee and the Friends Fellowship Council. As a result Yellow Springs Meeting in Ohio, attached to Indiana Yearly Meeting, and five new Meetings under Illinois have been established with a breath of new life in them all. Camp Ill-Ind-O, at Quaker Haven, Ind., has been a focus for young Friends, and a newssheet, *Friends Here and There,* furnished for some years a continuing thread of communication between the Meetings.

Both New York and Baltimore, of the eastern Yearly Meetings, were at first more interested in the Conference than was Philadelphia, which because of its greater size felt less need of it. New York has always been a strong Meeting with a number of fine leaders. Samuel Willets, the first president of the Swarthmore College Board of Managers, was an able member though never active in the Conference. Ellwood Burdsall, manufacturer, and Edward Cornell, an attorney, each served as clerk of the

Yearly Meeting. Many of these New York Friends, some of them in an excellent worldly position and active in the Meeting, did not want to be followers of Philadelphia just because it was so large. Partly for this reason, perhaps, their vigorous Yearly Meeting has been an energetic promoter of Conference work.

Baltimore, another large Yearly Meeting, has furnished valued guidance in the Conference. Dr. O. Edward Janney, already in 1900 president of the American Purity Alliance and in 1906 one of the organizers of the National Vigilance Committee, was its first chairman, remaining at the post for twenty years. Eli M. Lamb, as we have seen, took an important part in the First-day School Conference. Throughout Baltimore Yearly Meeting there was an active participation in philanthropic causes of all kinds as well as wholehearted support of the Conference. In recent years the Meeting has been fortunate in the devoted service given it by Bliss and LaVerne Forbush. Bliss Forbush went to Baltimore to act as secretary to the city Monthly Meeting and was subsequently made secretary of the Yearly Meeting. With little help except the great contribution made by his wife, he pumped new vitality into everything. Bliss Forbush was appointed chairman of Friends General Conference in 1941, serving eight years following the twenty-one-year term of fine leadership provided by Arthur C. Jackson of Philadelphia. Ability as a speaker, a friendly spirit, and knowledge of the Bible gained in courses at the University of Chicago Divinity School have made Bliss Forbush a leading Hicksite Friend throughout the Conference.

One of the important sectors of Baltimore Yearly Meeting is the group of Friends in Washington, D. C. The

SEVEN YEARLY MEETINGS AT WORK TOGETHER

Orthodox meeting on Irving Street was a pastoral meeting, the Hicksite meeting on I Street was unprogrammed. Both came into national prominence during the term of public office of Herbert Hoover, who was born an Iowa Five Years Meeting Friend. While he was in President Coolidge's Cabinet as Secretary of Commerce, he attended the I Street Meeting. As President, however, it was evident to him and all the Friends that his presence at an unprogrammed meeting for worship based on silence would create problems. There would be too large a proportion of curiosity-seekers with no understanding of silent worship, the necessary retinue of officials would be a detriment to the spirit of the simple meeting, and it would be difficult to restrain non-Friends from speaking, especially when they saw a good chance to get the ear of the President. Hoover shifted to Irving Street. The Friends there, without a pastor at the time, asked him if he had a preference as to who should be chosen. He proposed his old friend, Augustus T. Murray, Emeritus Professor of Greek at Stanford University, who agreed to come as *a* minister, but not *the* minister. Later the President suggested that in the national capital Friends should present an undivided front. A number of Friends were ready to act on the recommendation. Within a year the new Florida Avenue Meeting House was built for the use of Friends of all branches. For a while all three houses were operated, but later both of the older ones were sold. Florida Avenue has become a part of the new united Potomac Quarterly Meeting which in 1951 succeeded the former Fairfax (Hicksite) and the Potomac parts of Baltimore (Orthodox) Quarters. Potomac reports to both Baltimore Yearly Meetings, not yet united, but one more step has been taken on the road toward union.

The development of all the Hicksite Yearly Meetings was in one or another way connected with the Friends General Conference. The larger ones put their strength into the combined effort, the smaller ones were helped into new growth. The early search for pooled experience in the fields of religious education and philanthropic endeavor expanded into a full current of lesson material, shorter or longer periods of adult study, and planned extension work to stimulate the formation of new Friends' Meetings. The activities brought wider acquaintance among the various bodies and resulted in interaction with the larger Quaker world.

CHAPTER VI

Biennial Pilgrimage

None of the special programs of Friends General Conference, neither the work in the Yearly Meetings nor the religious education and philanthropic efforts, would have progressed as they did had it not been for the recurring stimulation of the large biennial conferences. The sessions that had started in 1894 and had developed into the united body at Chautauqua have continued to be landmarks of Conference history. Since 1900, through fifty-two years and two world wars the biennial sequence has been almost uninterrupted. In the first two and a half decades the conferences moved from one locality to another to energize the resident Friends and to promote as much personal acquaintance as possible with each other's meetings. After the important Chautauqua assembly in 1900 the places selected were, in order, Asbury Park, N. J., Toronto, Canada, Mountain Lake Park, Md., Winona Lake, Ind., Ocean Grove, N. J., Chautauqua again in 1912, Saratoga Springs, N. Y., Cape May, N. J., in 1916 and 1920, Richmond, Ind., and Ocean City, N. J., in 1924 and 1926, and then, beginning with 1928, continuously at Cape May. Only one break occurred. In 1918 the United States was deeply involved in World War I, transportation for civilians was restricted, and many Friends felt that the money which the Conference would cost should be contributed to the relief work being undertaken by the American Friends Service Committee, organized the previous year. Accordingly, an enlarged session of the Central Committee, held at George School, was substituted.

Friends thoroughly enjoyed themselves at these Conferences. Jane Rushmore attended most of them and recalls them in considerable detail. Generally speaking, lectures were of a high order, discussions lively, and there usually was a quota of amusing incidents that gave flavor. Dr. Janney gave himself a good deal of pleasure one year by marching through the special train shouting "Smoker ahead!" thus horrifying the delegates who in large measure still regarded smoking by men (of course for women it was at that time almost unheard of) as a reprehensible if not actually immoral practice. Then Dr. Janney gleefully explained that he referred to the train's soft-coal burning engine which was liberally besmirching everyone. He produced one surprise even to himself. As the train pulled out from Philadelphia he had sent to Richmond a telegram giving the final check-up of attendance. "On board one thousand. Eight without homes." On arrival he found their Richmond hosts in a frenzy, ransacking the city for beds and food. The telegram they received had read: "On board one thousand eight without homes."

The Richmond Friends had gone to a great deal of trouble to supply enough seats for the big crowd. Many new folding chairs had been procured and neatly varnished. The First-day meeting for worship was long, the day was hot. When meeting was broken and the Friends rose, the chairs rose with them. Next day every drugstore in Richmond was out of benzine.

The Conference went to Ocean Grove with the understanding that the city made no charge for the use of the big auditorium. When they arrived they were told that while there was no regular fee, those using the hall usually gave the Ocean Grove Assembly their Sunday collection. The Friends' committee, a little nonplussed, asked what this amounted to and were told "about $500." Since

BIENNIAL PILGRIMAGE

Friends never take collections and would find it particularly objectionable to do so at First-day meeting, the $500 was paid from the treasury, supplemented by some private contributions, and the Conference returned there no more.

One day at Ocean City, Jane found Charles F. Underhill, an active member of New York Yearly Meeting, clerk of its Representative Committee, and a public reader by profession, in a depressed state. This was surprising as he had just read a very good paper to the Conference. He remarked in his most tragic manner that this was the saddest day of his life. "Why?" asked Jane incredulously. "I toiled and sweated over my address, and then afterwards someone said to me, 'That was an excellent paper, Charles. Did thy wife write it?'"

Jane Rushmore began attending conferences in 1894 when she was a delegate from New York Yearly Meeting, as she continued to be at least four times more. After that she was for many years a representative from Philadelphia. In the printed record there are some characteristic remarks that she offered at Swarthmore during her second Conference which show how she could point up a too common weakness of any society. "We don't believe in indifference, any of us. We believe in zeal. We believe in it mightily, but we practice indifference just about as much as we believe in zeal. That is, we believe that a great many people ought to be zealous, and most of us believe that other people are a great deal better able to do the work and show the zeal than we are." Indifference, with its resultant inactivity, Jane challenged throughout the span of her work with Friends. She wanted to see people do something about their convictions, move forward, make better opportunities and use them. Indirectly she had stated at the 1896 Conference one of the great objectives of her later work with Friends: to stimulate and to guide the indifferent and the timid into fruitful action.

At the first setting up of the Friends General Conference in 1900, a step was taken full of portent for the future. An invitation was sent to John Wilhelm Rowntree of England to attend and deliver one of the major addresses. John William Graham had come entirely on his own personal concern four years before, as we have said, adventurously charging the Hicksite lair. Although by 1900 there were a number of Hicksites who had cordial personal acquaintances among the Orthodox and with a few English Friends, officially the isolation of almost seventy-five years was in effect unbroken. The Hicksite Yearly Meetings were not recognized by London, Arch Street, or the Five Years Meeting. Nevertheless they decided to experiment with this request. John Wilhelm Rowntree did not come, but he sent a paper on "The Personal Element in Religion" with a message quoted by the chairman that "he would have been very glad to have been here himself, but feared our climate at this time," undoubtedly an honest reason, as American summers are a terrifying prospect to the British. George A. Barton, professor of Biblical and church history at Bryn Mawr College, did appear with a lecture on "The Religious Use of the Bible," but he came not as an emissary from Arch Street Yearly Meeting of which he was then a member, but as a scholar who was also a Friend.

Although John Wilhelm Rowntree did not respond by journeying to Chautauqua, English Friends had been made aware of the existence of the new Friends General Conference. Moreover, the American Friends were not discouraged by the only partial success of their initial effort. For the Asbury Park Conference they invited John William

Graham, who responded with three addresses, making himself so popular with the attenders that he was asked to return for the 1904 Conference in Toronto. This time he brought with him a minute from his Monthly Meeting, endorsed by the Quarterly Meeting, a real step forward and a gratification to both him and the Conference. But, as he explained frankly, no minute from the Meeting for Sufferings. While his concern had the support of perhaps two-thirds of that Meeting, the minority prevented the unanimity which was necessary. The objectors were some evangelical Friends "who," in John William Graham's words, "did not very much approve of me, and did not very much approve of you, and did not think the conjunction of the two dangerous elements would be altogether satisfactory. . . . It was rather too much to take upon . . . the cautious shoulders of persons who have sat over 250 years doing very wise and careful things at Devonshire House."

At Toronto also appeared for the first time on a Conference program that great liberal spirit, Rufus M. Jones, already living within the area of Arch Street Yearly Meeting, but a member of New England Yearly Meeting (Five Years).

Cracks were appearing in the hard walls of cherished misunderstanding. Members of London Yearly Meeting who ventured to America enjoyed coming to the conferences and summer schools; Hicksite Friends found themselves liking English Friends. Herbert G. Wood and Douglas Pepler with their wives were an inspiring and also a fun-loving part of the summer-school week in 1907 at George School. In 1906 John Ashworth of Manchester attended the Mountain Lake Park Conference without a minute, but when he made his second visit in 1908 he was able to present at Winona Lake a minute from his Monthly Meeting endorsed by both the Quarterly Meeting and the Meeting for Sufferings, the first word from that body to Hicksite Friends.

Another significant visitor at Winona Lake was Cyrus W. Harvey of Wichita, Kansas, bringing with him a minute from Kansas Yearly Meeting (Five Years). The story of his growing interest in Friends of the other branch went back some ten years or more. At that time, he told the Conference, he had been asked to write a paper on "The Relation of Quakerism to Modern Thought." In preparing it

> I became intensely interested in what we have been accustomed to call the doctrine of the Inward Light, because of its wonderful ramifications in the development of modern philosophy and the new thought in modern theology. As I was studying this question I became aware through things that came to me in the preparation of that lecture, that the body of Friends that you represent held and has held for generations strongly, definitely, to the doctrine of the Inward Light. When I became aware of this and comprehended its meaning, the desire arose in my heart to cross the line and see what sort of people you were.

He managed to secure a minute from his Monthly Meeting allowing him to make a general visit to any who bear the name of Friends. He was a pioneer in penetrating the barrier after seventy-two years of separation. In the company of Edwin Pierce of Moorestown, N. J., he hesitantly ventured into the Meeting of Hicksite Friends of Philadelphia (presumably Yearly Meeting) for almost all the sessions, then New York for all sessions, and the same at Illinois. Now, in 1908, at Winona Lake he rejoiced in the increasing fellowship across the stern borders. The path was still rough and narrow; it was no wide boulevard.

But the way was open at last. Cyrus Harvey gave the closing address of the Conference on "A Spiritual Atonement."

Jane Rushmore took part in many of these Conferences. She gave a paper at Winona Lake on "Training Teachers for First-day Schools," and in 1910 at Ocean Grove one on "The Religious School." She was offering modern ideas of Bible interpretation.

> You ought not to study the Bible in small fragments, but take the long outlook of history. Especially is this true of the Old Testament. . . . Unless we are able to take it up with a fair degree of consecutiveness and cover the field pretty thoroughly, so that we get the long outlook of the development of the Hebrew life and religious feeling, we are going to come out with very untrue and one-sided conceptions.

She was also a member of the Central Committee. There she advocated discontinuing the expensive printing of verbatim reports of the Conferences in favor of subsidizing the *Friends Intelligencer* to print a supplement with full but not such overextended accounts; she urged using the money thus saved for better programs at the Conferences; she was pushing for the extension of the series of graded lesson leaves.

By 1912 the whole organization was on much firmer footing. The Advancement Committee had sent requests to the several Yearly Meetings to make up $3,000 a year for its use. The First-day School and Philanthropic Committee asked for regular appropriations also. The Yearly Meetings responded, even Philadelphia, which theretofore had supported the Conference only by voluntary contributions from interested members. Curiously, Race Street Yearly Meeting, upon whose property or that of immediately related bodies the Conference office has always had its various abodes, and from whose Central Bureau its publications have been issued, was the last of the six Hicksite groups to become officially a part of the Conference. Its relative size and strength (it was the largest of the six) kept it from feeling the same need as the others did. At last in 1912, when the request for Yearly Meeting money was granted, Race Street became a regular member of the Conference. The clerk of its Yearly Meeting and of its Representative Committee have for many years been ex-officio members of the Central Committee.

When the big gathering assembled at Chautauqua in 1912, there was John William Graham for the fourth time, bringing with him a copy of the London letter "To All Who Bear the Name of Friends in America." Whether John William Graham or the Conference was the happier at this markedly new gesture from London cannot be measured now. He also brought important news, confirmed by cable after he left England: the purchase of Swarthmoor Hall by Emma Abraham (a descendant of Judge and Margaret Fell) with the help of a group of sixteen Friends led by Dr. Thomas Hodgkin. Provision was made for the Society of Friends to have the right to purchase in the future; meanwhile the property would be preserved as a Quaker shrine.* The Conference sent a letter of appreciation to English Friends.

Nor was John William Graham the only English visitor to Chautauqua. A much younger man, Harry T. Silcock, had also traveled to America, carrying a minute which bore to the young Friends of this country the cordial greetings of the Young Friends Committee of London Yearly Meeting, signed by seventeen of them. Acquaintance was indeed ripening.

* In 1951 the Society of Friends in England obtained a lease of Swarthmoor Hall and expects to keep it open to visitors, according to the practice since Emma Abraham bought it.

BIENNIAL PILGRIMAGE

Two years later at Saratoga Springs another English Friend, Robert L. Simkin, gave an address on "The Work of Friends in West China." The long covert opposition of Hicksite Friends to the evangelistic work of missionaries in the foreign field broke down to the extent of having on the Conference program a representative of London Yearly Meeting's missionary group in China. Here a Hicksite prejudice was yielding, after slow acceptance of the idea that "advancement work" did not have all the connotations of "proselyting" in its bad sense.

But the overshadowing event of this Conference was the sudden death there of Henry W. Wilbur. Shocked by the loss of the man who had actively furthered the Conference and had inaugurated the Advancement Committee, the Friends felt deeply the obligation to carry forward his purposes. Just two years before he had been given the title of general secretary of the Conference.

A feeling had been growing that a permanent location for the biennial conferences was very desirable. The 1916 session at Cape May was so satisfactory that in 1920 a second experiment there convinced a number of the Central Committee that the answer had been found. Friends from the Middle West, however, wanted the stimulating presence of a wide assembly of their fellows, so Richmond, Ind., was again chosen for 1922. The local membership outdid itself in hospitality and was especially lavish with treats of watermelons, which made a splendid impression on the guests. On the special train going back east after the close of the meetings the passengers grew hot and thirsty. Suddenly a rumor of "Watermelon!" spread. It was discovered that Robert Seaman of New York and William C. Biddle had brought several of the Indiana treasures aboard and were cutting them in the smoking room, having first covered the floor with paper. "We had no other use for the smoking room, so we thought we'd eat watermelon in it," said Robert Seaman.

The heat of Indiana persuaded the Committee to return to the seacoast, and Ocean City, N. J., was the scene of both the 1924 and the 1926 conferences. This move was so popular that in 1926 the attendance reached twelve hundred, among whom were ninety children. The New Jersey shore had won out over all competitors. Cape May offered such attractive conditions and improvements for 1928 that the Conference returned there, with the result that this town has been the home of the gatherings for every session since.

With a stabilized place of meeting, the programs also took on an orderly, progressive development. Attendance increased. Friends from other branches or other countries were less the exception, more the regularly expected fellow attenders.

Young people had a more important place. When Jane Rushmore was chairman of the program committee for 1920, a plan which began at Saratoga merely in providing care for children was extended to a regularly organized period for the youngest members. Emma Wallace and Elsie Oakford, assisted by four other teachers, all from Friends' schools, set up morning classes on the beach. For many recent years under the able direction of Vesta Haines, this program, called the Junior Conference, has become an important feature of every gathering. Later a high-school section with special activities for teen-agers was added, and now the Young Friends' headquarters has more and more not only arranged special meetings and activities of its own, but has seen its members take more part in the larger program, especially at the round-table discussions. The topics for these, closely allied to the subjects of the main addresses, include Bible study, principles of Friends, religious and secular education, peace, and various forms of social service.

For all age groups the instituting of round tables has proved a valuable technique as the size of the Conferences has increased. Problems always exist for Friends gathered in very large numbers. George Fox, to be sure, preached to thousands, but in latter days the desire to have many take part in discussion, feel responsibility for expression in the meeting for worship, and experience the close fellowship of the spirit that can best exist in small groups requires the frequent breaking up of a great congregation into lesser units. Therefore, in addition to the round tables, there are of recent years a number of small daily meetings for worship which often provide a greater intensity of silence and communion. With attendance now running at about two thousand, approximately 10 per cent of the total membership, and programs well arranged for all ages, the biennial Conferences have an established and valuable place in welding together Friends from distant Meetings and of diverse views.

Closely connected in interest to the whole General Conference, though not under its direct control, is the *Friends Intelligencer*. This weekly publication has appeared uninterruptedly for more than one hundred years and is the unofficial organ of the Hicksite Yearly Meetings. It is reported that in 1844 a young Philadelphia Friend named Chapman, by profession a printer, enlisted the coöperation of Edward Parrish (later the first president of Swarthmore College) and shortly they announced an association of Friends who would act as editors of the new periodical. All were members of Philadelphia Yearly Meeting: Dr. John Griscom, Dillwyn and Isaac Parrish, William M.

Dorsey, William P. Sharpless, and Morris L. Hallowell. Some years later, in 1853, this group was replaced by five women Friends: Harriet J. Moore, Jane Johnson, Anna A. Townsend, Deborah Fisher Wharton, and Susanna M. Parrish. Of these women, Jane Johnson had had useful experience.* She had started the first First-day school in Philadelphia, had published in 1844 a little book, *Early Impressions, or Evidences of the Secret Operations of the Divine Witness in the Minds of Children,* which contained, in old-fashioned language, simple accounts of incidents in the childhood of a number of early Friends. She later wrote other small books, some of the earliest material for First-day schools, and sent contributions to *Scattered Seeds,* a magazine for children. She, Deborah Wharton, Susanna Parrish, and Anna Townsend had all been members, along with others, of a committee to establish Meeting libraries and loan books to them, so they were well accustomed to working together when they became editors of the *Intelligencer.*

The women's board existed for many years. As the older members resigned or died, they were succeeded by Helen G. Longstreth, Susan Roberts, Louisa J. Roberts, Lydia H. Hall, Rachel W. Hillborn. The board devoted a full day each week to the paper, reading aloud all the original contributions. The material presented was largely essays, poetry, and religious articles. Advertisements of Friends' schools were carried. From them we learn that in the 1860's the tuition was $60 per twenty-week term at a boarding school, with painting or foreign languages five dollars extra. A boys' school announced that "no game of chance, like Dice, Domino or Cards will be tolerated," and

* See account by Marguerite Hallowell, "Jane Johnson," in *Quaker Torchbearers* (Philadelphia, 1943), pp. 154 ff.

a girls' school assured patrons that "no accomplishment inconsistent with Friends' principles" would be taught.

Because of the restricted contents of the *Intelligencer*, another publication was started during the period of Jane Rushmore's childhood called the *Journal*, which carried news of First-day school unions, accounts of Friends' meetings, comments on public affairs. Beginning in 1885 under the editorship of Howard M. Jenkins the two papers were merged, the group of women becoming associate editors. Howard Jenkins at once enlarged the scope of the *Friends Intelligencer and Journal* with material on Friends' testimonies, especially peace. He tried to draw all the Hicksite Meetings closer together and to cultivate some acquaintance with the other branch by a column called "News of Arch Street Friends." His death left Lydia Hall and Rachel Hillborn to continue by themselves, though they soon were fortunate in procuring the help of Charles F. Jenkins as business manager. Regular editors began with R. Barclay Spicer, who served as editor for seven years, and Henry Ferris, who served for five. Then Sue C. Yerkes became head for twenty-one years, followed immediately in 1943 by William Hubben.*

According to its new articles of incorporation, adopted in 1953, a certain number of the governing body of the *Friends Intelligencer* will be appointed by the General Conference, others by the supporting group of *Friends Intelligencer* Associates. The paper's constant growth in circulation is evidence of general satisfaction with it, as is the financial aid given it by Friends throughout the Conference area.

During World War I a group who did not like the

* See account by Katherine L. Smyth in *Friends Intelligencer* for Eleventh Month 20, 1943, pp. 769 ff.

pacifist emphasis of the *Intelligencer* started a new paper called the *Quaker*. It had a good format and appearance, opening well with Marcia Doane as editor. She was the daughter of Wilson M. Doane, an Indianapolis lawyer and prominent Indiana Friend. Two years later she was killed in an automobile accident and the *Quaker* was given up.

Looked at as an unfolding story of many manifestations during more than fifty years, Friends General Conference has shown in Jane Rushmore's view a steady strengthening in the vital concerns of a religious society. Beginning as an opportunity for the several Yearly Meetings to know each other better, it was strictly self-contained. Those interested in First-day schools, "philanthropic labor," and education conferred and compared. They attracted a number of Friends; all had a good time together and were stimulated by finding themselves in a large group instead of feeling, as they did at home, that they were a tiny minority in their community. Then their small local Meetings began to receive definite help through the Advancement Committee, and their members were encouraged to attend institutes, summer schools, or take courses at Woolman School, all initiated by the Conference. In these schools and in the programs of the biennial Conferences definite stress was placed on the religious life, Bible study, and an outreach to others. Lecturers from outside groups of Friends gradually widened the acquaintance with English and American Quakerism.

The remarkably devoted chairmen who led the Conference through this era were O. Edward Janney and Arthur C. Jackson, the first for twenty, the second for twenty-one years, followed by Bliss Forbush and now George A. Walton. These chairmen have been ably assisted in the office by the imagination and drive of Henry W. Wilbur and by the careful follow-up work of J. Barnard Walton, who became everyone's friend, welcomed throughout all the Yearly Meetings as a visible bond of love and unity. Since his retirement in 1951 he has been succeeded by Earle Edwards, who hopes for still greater integration and strength of combined spiritual resources. Barnard Walton is now the field secretary.

As the Cape May gatherings have grown, as the visiting of the various meetings by traveling Friends has been encouraged, as the religious education material has improved with local conferences, study groups and institutes, and as, in coöperation with Friends Fellowship Council, new groups of seekers have been helped to form new Meetings, the influence of the Conference is everywhere apparent. While Friends have had a strong distrust of figures as a measure of progress, they do recognize that the value of the General Conference is at least in some part reflected by the fact that after its advent the long downward trend in membership among the Hicksite Yearly Meetings stopped. Then there slowly started an upward curve. The total membership of the Conference Meetings is now in the neighborhood of 19,000 of which Philadelphia Yearly Meeting numbers about 12,000.

With the entire history of the Conference, Jane Rushmore has been familiar. Her connection with it began during her teaching years at London Grove; it continued for the period of her work at Starr Center, and went on all through her career with Philadelphia Yearly Meeting. Her time of greatest usefulness to the Conference was concurrent with her professional and voluntary service at Fifteenth and Race streets, for there she had at hand the tools to work with. Her office did the major part of the

Conference printing and distribution. The fact that the Conference office and hers were adjacent made possible constant interchange of information that was advantageous to both.

It is her observation now that increasingly a marked emphasis has been placed on the quest for spiritual values. Meetings for worship receive special attention, roundtable conferences seek earnestly to understand the motivating force which leads Friends into humanitarian service. The spiritual temperature, she says, has definitely risen.

She has reason to know. She directed the work done for the Conference at Friends Central Bureau. She served on the Conference Philanthropic, First-day School, Education, and Advancement Committees. As clerk of Philadelphia Yearly Meeting and then clerk of its Representative Committee she was an ex-officio member of the Conference Central Committee for a long term of years. Although she felt that she stayed far too long in General Conference councils, her voice was never heard except in clear thinking and pungent phrasing. Moreover, in the last years she had become an elder statesman of extremely wide experience among Friends, for she had spent some thirty-four years in the very center of all the activities of Race Street Yearly Meeting.

CHAPTER VII

At the Hub

The important assistance given to the General Conference for many years by Friends Central Bureau has been repeatedly mentioned. As it developed, that institution, externally merely an office for the convenience of the Yearly Meeting, has actually greatly extended the whole usefulness of Philadelphia Friends. In all its major aspects the Bureau has been the creation of Jane P. Rushmore.

Talk of it began in 1911 when William C. Coles, chairman of Philadelphia's Philanthropic Committee, was growing impatient because work was being hampered by lack of clerical help. He discovered that the First-day School Committee was irked by the same lack, and that while the Education Committee had a full-time officer in Ellen H. E. Price, she had no adequate working space. The persons looking for a way to deal with this problem had a strong supporter in Herbert P. Worth of West Chester, a man of action and chairman of the General Conference Committee on First-day Schools. He wanted facilities for distributing lesson leaves since Henry Wilbur's small office for advancement work was in no way equipped to handle lesson material. These Friends decided to make a united appeal to the Yearly Meeting for an office and a secretary. They had talked a good deal ahead of time and counted among their supporters Mary H. Whitson, James H. Atkinson, Susan W. Janney, Benjamin F. Battin, Robert Pyle, and Frank Bartram. They hoped that their novel proposal might win enough favor for a committee to be appointed to consider the matter and bring in recommendations the following year.

As anticipated, many Friends were very doubtful. The work of the Yearly Meeting had always been carried by volunteers as a religious duty. The new office meant the introduction of professionalism, its head might soon become the paid organizer and leader of the Society, voluntary service would largely cease. Friends might lose sight of one of the basic principles of their organization—that of the personal carrying by each member of a share in the whole work of the Meeting. With what Jane calls "great perspiration of soul" the Yearly Meeting grappled with the problem. Those who believed that clerical help was no infiltration of subversive anti-Quakerism strove to reassure the conservatives. Pleas for wider effectiveness of three important phases of Yearly Meeting work had to be given due weight. At last the Meeting, considerably shaken out of its accustomed quiet routine, appeared ready for decision. No vote was taken, of course. To the surprise of even the strongest advocates of a central office, the Yearly Meeting agreed that the three committees should select seven members each, which twenty-one Friends should have authority to give careful thought to the setting up of a secretarial bureau under an appropriation of $1500.

The Bureau Committee went into action forthwith. Naming Benjamin F. Battin as chairman, they laid out their needs, their limitations and possibilities, and they began their search for an office and a director. Herbert Worth, who with Ellwood Hollingshead and Mary H. Whitson made up the subcommittee to select a secretary, received a strong letter from Robert Pyle, stating in his most forceful way his conviction that the one person preëminently suitable for the post of director was his former teacher and his family's long-time friend, Jane P. Rushmore. Jane was no stranger to Herbert Worth. First-day school work in the Conference and the Yearly Meeting had made them well acquainted. She may well have been his own nomination. Perhaps others suggested her also. In any event the committee approached her.

She did not accept immediately. Starr Center was an established enterprise where her position was secure. She would cut her salary in half if she changed her job and she would face an uncertain future. On the other hand, her friend Susan Wharton was giving up her close connection with the Center. Jane had grown interested in Quaker outreach especially through her work with the Conference. Above all, she found it hard to resist the opportunity of an experiment whose future scope she could not foresee but which seemed to have possibilities of growth. She agreed to begin work on October 1, 1911. Her salary was to be $1000 a year.

The new undertaking would be conducted on the large mid-city property at Fifteenth and Race streets, the recognized center for Yearly Meeting interests. In 1911 nearly all the buildings in the block bounded by Race, Fifteenth, Cherry, and Mole streets were in actual use by Friends. The large meeting house, built in 1856, stood facing Race Street in the middle of the enclosure but was set far back from the tall iron fence. There was room between for a good-sized plot of grass breaking the otherwise complete brick paving of the yard. The quiet desired for the house of worship was protected by a continuous line of buildings on Fifteenth Street. Friends' Central School, four stories high, occupied the southeast corner of Fifteenth and Race streets. Between it and the Young Friends Association at Fifteenth and Cherry were several small residences, all but two of which were owned by the Meeting or by individual Friends. The elementary school was housed in a generous-sized structure at the Race and Mole streets corner. A wall hid the row of tiny dwellings running the rest of the way along the narrow lane of Mole Street to Cherry. On Cherry Street another high brick wall, pierced by iron gates, completed the seclusion given to the great meeting house. A visitor might enter the precincts through the gates on Race Street, or those on Cherry, or through one of the schools, or through a covered passage leading from Fifteenth Street between Friends' Central School and the home of the superintendent of the property. To one coming into the spacious yard an appreciable sense of separation from the busy city was always apparent.

Title to different segments of this real estate was variously held by several Quaker groups. The Cherry Street end of the meeting house with its smaller auditorium was owned by the Yearly Meeting, connecting by committee rooms with the larger Race Street section owned by the Monthly Meeting. During most of the year the Cherry Street side was kept closed and, says Jane, "seemed to have no function except to collect dust." She comments further:

> One week in the year, when Yearly Meeting came around, the men were in glorious possession. Here they held sway until 1924 when the men's and women's meetings joined. Masculine independence of feminine rule was established when the men refused to have their clock record daylight-saving time. Yearly Meeting on the Race Street side began at ten o'clock; on the Cherry Street side at nine. The men adjourned at eleven in order to be on hand for lunch which was served at noon, DST, by the hospitality committee of Race and Green Street Monthly Meetings.

On Yearly Meeting First-day, crowds of Friends came to worship in both meeting houses and in the auditorium of Friends' Central School, and afterward in warm May

The Meeting House at Fifteenth and Race Street

AT THE HUB

sunshine the yard was filled with a lingering throng milling happily about, seeking acquaintances from distant points come to town for the annual gathering.

As the years passed the aspect changed: the schools were removed to Overbrook; offices were established in the elementary school building and in the Cherry Street Meeting House; and the Young Friends Association headquarters were remodeled into the Whittier Hotel. But the location has remained modestly imposing. Religious, educational, philanthropic, and social interests of Friends have been fostered here for nearly a century.

For the use of Friends Central Bureau in 1911 two rooms had been secured at 150 North Fifteenth Street, on the first floor of one of the small houses which helped form the eastern boundary of the Yearly Meeting premises. The building was owned by a Race Street Monthly Meeting member, Isaac H. Clothier. The back room was assigned to Ellen H. E. Price for the work of the Yearly Meeting's Education Committee. The front one was prepared for the new Bureau. Furniture was bought by the Representative Committee, which would also share in the coming services. Simplicity was the keynote. Two desks were provided, four chairs, one typewriter, and a "long-distance telephone." Nothing more. The executive and her typist might each seat a visiting Friend; further amenities or working materials would be supplied by conversation and the desk drawers. When Jane insinuated herself into the diminutive room in October it was clear that the restraint of the furnishings committee was not entirely mistaken. Finding a few books for the use of the First-day School Committee, she piled them on the floor. Susan W. Janney, a member of the Bureau Committee, saw these one day with disapproval. "What are the books doing on the floor?" she asked. "There isn't any other place to put them," Jane explained. Susan soon persuaded someone to give a bookcase, which was squeezed in, and the Bureau's lending library was established. Five books were loaned the first year.

The minute under which the Bureau was operating read: "The secretary is to have a general view of conditions existing in the Yearly Meeting, to make a study of the practical problems, and so organize and coordinate the work that individuals may spend their efforts to the greatest advantage." When she had been first interviewed about the position Jane had said, "I have one good qualification. I have the ability to say No." Whatever was office business to serve the Yearly Meeting she undertook; what was not, she refused. Jane made the decisions, using as her guide the Yearly Meeting's own determination that no part of its prerogatives should be assumed by the Bureau, but only the mechanics of carrying out the Meeting's work. The other boundary to the activities was the budget. Even in 1911 an appropriation of $1500 could not possibly have covered rent, two salaries, and office expenses had the Bureau not opened late in the fiscal year (May to May). To stretch the money over eight months was close work.

Some financial assistance came from Friends General Conference. At the beginning, the Bureau Committee had been charged to write to the Conference First-day School Committee and other organizations inviting them to make use of the services offered and to assist in their support. Immediately an arrangement was made with the Conference by which it paid to have the office business of its First-day School Committee transacted and its lessons printed and distributed.

AT THE HUB

For the Yearly Meeting the first business in hand was to organize existing material and resources more effectively. A card list was begun of the total membership of Race Street Yearly Meeting. A few local Meetings furnished their lists cheerfully, but some had to be persuaded with assurances that they would be confidential and never used commercially. One Meeting thought it not worth while as an undertaking; the list is changing every week, they said. Eventually all complied. The plan was hard to initiate, but is now a valuable reference file kept up to date annually. The efforts for accuracy made by the Monthly Meetings and the Bureau had some adverse effects statistically for several years, but with paper losses written off a sounder picture emerged. Several Meetings actually found it to their advantage, for the quota of financial support to the Yearly Meeting, based on membership, was more precisely apportioned and the justice of the assessments won better collections.

While this was in progress the work of servicing the committees also began. Those most interested in setting up the Bureau at once asked to have their notices sent out. "Certainly," said Jane. "What about the postage?" "Just send the bill to our committee and it will be refunded." "But I have no money with which to buy the stamps, and the post office does not give credit to committees." So James H. Atkinson, a professional accountant, already treasurer of numerous Quaker organizations, among them the Central Bureau, set up the first petty cash system. Not more than two dollars was ever advanced by the Bureau at that time, enough to send out notices of regular meetings. In all these small and seemingly unimportant beginnings Jane was extremely careful that every step should be clearly in a direction that would not cause later confusion but would lead into a useful pattern. Among the first rules adopted was one that the office should never reply to any inquiry with "I don't know." The Bureau was set up for service and if answers were not available, the staff should always say, "I don't have that information at hand just now, but I'll look it up for thee."

In her personal preparation for her position, Jane had read all the reports of Yearly Meeting committees for the previous thirty years. She found that not much accomplishment was recorded, minutes were sometimes far from clear, with decisions hazy or blurred, and the records kept in all sorts of books. The Bureau's offer to type the minutes in itself induced better written and more unified forms. The same thing happened with committee personnel. Members were practically never taken off a committee except by definite request, for the plan of definite terms of service had not yet been adopted. Lists were cluttered with names of inactive Friends; addresses had not been overhauled for years. Some people did not even know they were supposed to be on certain committees. Bringing order out of this confusion was a major task.

A third undertaking of the Bureau was the printing of the *Friends' Almanac,* a booklet, by then much out of date, of locations and times of holding all meetings in the Friends General Conference. With the facilities which the new Bureau had for gathering current facts from the Meetings, in 1913 the Representative Committee, through the Bureau, put out the *Friends Year Book* (later the *Calendar*) containing a large amount of material about Meetings, their First-day schools, Friends Associations, names of clerks, and so forth. Since 1949, when Arch Street Friends joined in its publication, it has been made *The Calendar* of all Meetings in the Philadelphia area.

AT THE HUB

A *Book of Meetings* was printed from time to time, listing all the Meetings in the Conference and how to reach them, and the committees of Philadelphia Yearly Meeting. It also offered the names, adressses, and officers of a number of organizations which were started by Friends and predominantly Friendly though not under the direct care of a Race Street Meeting, such as the American Friends Service Committee, or, dating from an earlier century, Friends Charity Fuel Association, and The Female Association of Philadelphia for the Relief of the Sick and Infirm Poor with Clothing (for many years, beginning soon after its founding in 1828, "Etcetera" was added as the last word in the title, signifying bread distributed or blankets loaned for the winter season and then recalled!). Since the Friends World Committee now prints a directory of all Meetings, it seems unlikely that the listing of Conference Meetings will appear again.

As the Yearly Meeting sessions came around the new Bureau proved to be of great service. It typed the minutes from the clerk's notes and it took over the preparation and printing of the *Extracts* which were taken from the minutes and circulated among the local Meetings. Then it began investigating how many copies of the *Extracts* were actually used and how many just lay on the back benches and window sills. Thus considerable waste was eliminated. A number of years later the practice was begun of printing in advance the reports to be submitted by standing committees to the Yearly Meeting. These were used at its sessions as well as in the local Meetings.

Jane was still not satisfied that the Bureau was fulfilling its mission in spite of all the services it was rendering to committees, visitors, and through the mails. She felt that she herself must be really acquainted with local conditions.

So after working in the office six days a week, she spent most of her Sundays visiting Meetings. In the first few years she went at least once to every Meeting within the Race Street boundaries except three: Schuylkill, then closed; Greenwich, which at that time had only five attenders; and Orange Grove, Cal., quite out of reach. But Millville, Pa., and Camden, Del., each roughly one hundred miles from Philadelphia, she reached by none too convenient public conveyances. A local resident of Millville told her that the little "S. B. & B." Railroad which served Millville was known as "Sundry Bumps and Bruises."

It was important that the local Meetings should feel not only that the Bureau was useful to the Yearly Meeting and its committees, but that the office had something to offer them individually which they could use. The most obvious service was in connection with their First-day schools. The schools were ordering lesson material rather at random. Indeed in one of the western Meetings Jane discovered that when the First-day school assured her that they had graded lessons they meant that they used the first quarter in the first class, the second quarter in the next class, and so on. It was evident that steps must be taken to help schools understand how to use the material furnished. Here the Bureau offered valuable counsel.

For seven years it thus built itself into greater usefulness. By 1918 it was so cramped for space that some change had to be made. Herbert P. Worth, who had the year before succeeded Benjamin Battin as chairman of the Bureau Committee, agreed that the time had come for expansion. The consent of the Yearly Meeting was obtained to wall off a part of the east end of the Cherry Street Meeting House, under the gallery, to give space that would make possible a second assistant for Jane, and also a desk for the secretary of the new Young Friends Movement.

This latter organization was only two years old. The Young Friends Associations, which had been started thirty years before on the initiative of Charles M. Stabler, Isaac Roberts, and others, had spread rapidly through the Yearly Meeting and had served a good purpose in providing social mingling and acquaintance through literary, musical, or study programs. But in time their special attraction appeared to be for middle-aged Friends.

Finally Rachel Knight, a gifted young member of Abington Meeting, went to England to study and came home filled with desire to get the really young people into action. Largely through her incentive the Young Friends Movement was organized in 1916. Two years later Eliza Ambler (Foulke) became its first secretary.

Eliza found it her great good fortune to be situated so near to Jane Rushmore, for in Jane the new young executive recognized a remarkable teacher of administration, instructor in Quaker background, and mine of information on persons and events. Jane told Eliza, "Young people won't get on a sinking ship. Thee'll have to be going somewhere." Jane was a firm believer in young people; she expected much of them and they rose to her standards. Eliza is sure that the Young Friends Movement owes much of its good start to Jane. On the other hand, Jane saw in Eliza a very able leader throughout her five years' service. She was a natural organizer. She started week-end pilgrimages of young people to various Meetings. On these trips the young Friends were well shuffled as they came from and went to distant points, they had a project, they had a good time, they were stimulating to the Meetings visited. A number of people who have given memorable service to the Society of Friends in their mature life, such as Anna Griscom (Elkinton) and Thomas A. Foulke (who married the Young Friends' secretary), enthusiastically began with important work among their young contemporaries.

This lively group did not like divisions. From the beginning they had many activities with a similar, though originally somewhat older, group from Arch Street. With them they attended joint conferences at Earlham and Westtown, and in 1930 they became one united organization in Philadelphia. This completely united body has undoubtedly had a strong effect on the growing trend toward union between the two Yearly Meetings. Headquarters for the Young Friends have always been within or adjoining the Friends Central Bureau.

Further moves of the Bureau followed the one in 1918, always to gain more space. In 1921 a move was made to 154 North Fifteenth Street, a small house belonging to Philadelphia Monthly Meeting and rented from them. Here the Bureau had use of the entire building, and here they remained until 1928. By this time the men and women had united for Yearly Meeting and the Race Street side was used for all sessions. Consequently, extensive alterations were possible to create the present offices in Cherry Street Meeting House. At this time Jane Rushmore urged the Yearly Meeting Trustees to take quarters here and build vaults in the basement, thus saving rental charges elsewhere. But the vaults were never built and the Trustees did not move in until 1950, when further changes were made converting the gallery also into usable office space.

As the growing Bureau received more and more requests for aid, Jane's policies, established early, showed themselves to be wise. In the main they were, first, to relieve committees of routine work and to do everything possible to promote volunteer activity; second, to establish a center of information about Friends and of information that Friends want; third, to eliminate waste and duplication. To a group like the Society of Friends the last of these so strongly commended itself that it alone could practically silence any criticism of the Bureau.

Where criticism arose at the beginning it concerned the old fear that the office would expect to do everything for the Yearly Meeting. But as committee officers and members came to the Bureau they soon found in its director a sympathetic listener, a counselor and adviser, but definitely not an executive to do their work for them. Her fertile and practical mind often made suggestions which they could carry out, or stimulated them to discovering something more active to do. When they came to her baffled with a problem, she did not demonstrate their error out of her experience. She persuaded them to talk until they had shown up the entire issue. Her probing finally made them analyze the question so completely that they themselves knew the answer. She says now that people nearly always know how they ought to decide things if they see the problem clearly. "They came to me and thought they had fine advice. Actually they hadn't had any. They found their own answers." Jane's skill as a teacher was still being turned to account.

As a source of information the list of correct names and addresses was only a start. Files were built up which amassed and classified a considerable accumulation of material on religious and secular education and the testimonies of the Society of Friends. The staff could produce material for preparing debates, or writing papers, or supplementing religious teaching, or serving as the basis for local committee action. Nowadays the answer to an inquirer is seldom, "I'll be glad to look that up for thee." Usually it is right at hand.

Because the Yearly Meeting was and is conservative, care was taken to proceed with great regularity. "Many enthusiastic, earnest, and perhaps right workers aren't willing to move through regular channels, and people don't trust them," Jane observes now. "I tried to respect all honest conservatism, but occasionally I liked to jolt people who love ruts out of the old and into new ones which are just as comfortable. They go a little farther as they move."

So much increased service could not be accomplished without increases in staff and equipment. Slowly labor-saving machines were added; slowly the number of assistants rose. In 1924 when field work in education and religious education was undertaken, a fourth assistant was added. By 1936 the staff numbered six, one of them a secretary for social service. The Yearly Meeting never refused a request for more money for the Bureau. Friends knew that Jane would not ask an increase for herself; it all went into larger services whose worth had been demonstrated. Indeed, although her salary was raised over the initial figure, Jane always had very moderate compensation, so little that some Friends were ashamed for the Yearly Meeting, and more would have been had they known the facts. But for Jane personal recognition was not important; her idea was to subordinate the Bureau and its staff to the committees, the office acting as a general coördinator.

It did become evident, however, that a useful purpose was served if staff members were appointed on various of the Yearly Meeting committees. Such appointments were valuable to both sides; the committees had immediate access to knowledge gained in the field by the Bureau personnel, and the office knew the reactions and attitudes of committee members.

Specific services were added by the Bureau from time to time, such as selling a few books of special interest to Friends and furnishing marriage certificates. The Bureau was given charge of completed minute books of all kinds, which were stored in the fireproof room of the meeting house. Here they were considered safe but were not easily accessible. Therefore when by the gift of Clement M. Biddle a fireproof building for the Friends Historical Library was opened at Swarthmore College, many records were transferred there, to the greater satisfaction of all who wanted to use them. Jane has been on the staff of honorary custodians since this library was started.

In addition to serving the Yearly Meeting's committees and Philadelphia Quarterly and Monthly Meetings, assembling information, statistics, and offering counsel, the Bureau has carried a large, continuing program of printing and distribution. The series of lesson leaves, which had been issued since 1885, was the first in this line. Then came the publication of the *First-day School Bulletin*, beginning in 1916. For the work on both of these the General Conference made an appropriation which covered printing and mailing. In 1917 the Bureau took over the business management and circulation of *Scattered Seeds*, a monthly magazine for small children. This little paper started by Lydia Hall in 1869 contained suitable stories, verses, and pictures for children in First-day schools. There was nothing like it available to Friends, and it was for many years a very helpful addition to the material for primary classes. After Lydia Hall's death, her daughters Alice Hall Paxson and Abby Mary Hall Roberts published it, and they continued as its editors after the Bureau assumed the business details. In 1935, with the advent of considerably more reading material suitable for young children, *Scattered Seeds* was discontinued.

Mention has been made of the first small hymnal produced for the General Conference in 1919; several subsequent and larger editions were printed, involving a great deal of work with copyright and other technical matters. Somewhat less difficult was the printing of a book of religious poems and prose selections called *The Higher Life*. This appeared in two volumes and has been useful to Friends who want to know where to find inspiring words, especially in times of affliction or death. A somewhat similar book called *Founding a Home,* prepared in 1946 but now out of print, also served a helpful purpose. These two compilations were produced under the authority of the Representative Committee, but the Bureau did all the work of preparing and distributing them. It also carried through the regular printing and distribution of the *Messenger,* a small periodical of the Representative Committee now reaching six thousand copies per issue, and the *Courier,* prepared for the Committee on Education.

As early as 1924 Jane began to reduce the time that she spent in the Bureau. At intervals over the next twenty years she slowly lessened her official number of days per week until in 1945 she resigned all her duties, turning over to Marguerite Hallowell the charge of the office and to Richmond P. Miller the work in the field.

The expansion of the Bureau during her thirty-four years as its head attests her power of organization, promotion, and persuasiveness. From a staff of two to a staff of nine; from a budget of $1500 to one of $24,000; from five books loaned in 1911 to more than 1350 taken out in 1952; from assisting five committees at the start to working for eighteen Yearly Meeting committees, their twenty subcommittees, plus serving Philadelphia Quarterly and Monthly Meetings, the clerk and the treasurer of Philadelphia Yearly Meeting, the clerk and the Planning Committee of Philadelphia General Meeting, and the Religious Education Committee of Friends General Conference; mimeographing material that now amounts to more than 16,000 pieces per year—all of this growth accomplished to the general satisfaction of the membership attests to Jane Rushmore's power of organization and to the rightness of the pattern she set.

There has been a constant effort to increase production without increasing costs. In one of her reports (1941) Jane remarked,

> The centralized control of everybody's time and use of the same office equipment enables the Bureau to accomplish a much greater amount of work with a smaller expenditure of money than would be the case under an organization . . . where every office is independent of every other office and a larger number of secretaries are paid.

But, as everyone in the Yearly Meeting knows, technical and material services were only a part of Jane's importance as secretary of the Bureau. In the first place she trained her assistants by giving them a background of Friends' principles, a history of the Meetings, and acquaintance with local situations. Therefore, as she withdrew, their knowledge was adequate to carry on. Their initiative was encouraged and their suggestions for increasing efficiency of the work were gladly received and considered. "A spirit of mutual coöperation and helpfulness was an important asset in making the Bureau valuable," Jane said. "The evolution of the work in the office and field was largely due to the intelligence and loyalty of the Bureau force."

With her unusual memory she became such an encyclopedia of information that she was consulted by almost everyone who had any business whatever in the Yearly Meeting. She could have manipulated every one of its committees by her favorable or adverse suggestions for its membership. Indeed as she came to see how much power lay in her hands, she recognized it as a danger. No one person should have so much influence in the Society of Friends, she said. Therefore she tried her best to keep her hands off local affairs. Friends were sometimes annoyed when she would not take action which they thought would be helpful. In her mind it was still more helpful to put the responsibility on others. What she did try to do was to encourage more people to assume their share of the work, to stimulate them into new thinking appropriate to new situations. She tried not to dictate judgments, but to be sure that those who should make them saw all the way around the question and had all the facts in hand before they made their decisions, so that their action was mature and well reasoned. One Friend, summing up her work at the Bureau, says: "She tried to hold the various elements of the Yearly Meeting in balance, check false starts, prevent trouble before it arose. A measure of her success is that she had the confidence of both as conservative a man as Alfred Moore and as radical a one as Jesse Holmes."

Not that everyone agreed with her. No one could be so positive a force in such a key place without meeting opposition. Some took issue with her on her basic reasoning. Some were occasionally hurt by her incisive mind and decided views. Some saw that she was apt to be impatient with people who didn't get things done, although she would not tolerate efforts to displace any who had served faithfully. Some thought her actions were at times arbitrary. But there could be none who questioned her single-minded devotion to the Yearly Meeting, her lack of self-seeking, her constant generosity in time and strength to all that concerned the fundamentals of her religious society and the fellowship of those who were within its bounds.

CHAPTER VIII

As a Reasonable Service

Jane Rushmore's professional activity at the Central Bureau, plus her contribution to Friends General Conference through its several divisions and its Central Committee, made up only a fraction of her work for the Yearly Meeting. She also took part in a long list of committees, often for long terms of appointment. While she was still at Starr Center, she was in 1908 made a member of the Yearly Meeting Committee on First-day schools. She was also at the same time "general secretary," or volunteer adviser, of the same committee of the Conference. Close to the center of her interest as this work always had been, she began with these appointments to learn more of the actual conditions in the field. The lesson leaves were not adequate, she saw, and there was a great dearth of trained teachers; in fact the Friends did not know very much about how to produce good First-day schools.

The Philadelphia committee charged with this concern was, therefore, beginning what was to be a long-sustained effort to develop First-day schools that were really schools and not just amateur attempts with more or less appropriate readings and stories. Again it must be recalled that for a long period Friends were opposed to definite religious instruction of this type and so lagged far behind other denominations in its cultivation. But a real start in grading was initiated—not too successfully because sometimes there were but a few children in the school and these with a wide age range. A fairly continuous stream of new material was being prepared, whose quality Jane at once sought to improve. There were usually two sets of lessons issued per year as a quarterly series, one for adults and one for children. Before long Jane was writing a good number of them, some bearing her name but most of them unsigned. An especially popular series, "An Elementary Study of the Bible," gave a survey of the whole book for adults untrained in Bible study. Experts were warned away from it. Jane made no pretension of being a Biblical scholar but she was entirely able to write an adequate general introduction to the significance of the Scriptures. Other courses on interpretation of the Bible, origins of Quakerism, studies in vital religion, on religion as affecting such areas of life as racial tensions, scientific advances, problems of nationalism, basic freedoms, all flowed from her pen. One series proved so useful that it was enlarged and printed as a book, *Testimonies and Practice of the Society of Friends*. Its purpose, it states, is to provide "a ready reference book covering the religious profession, social concern, educational interest and the organization of Friends," the presentation being of course that of Race Street Yearly Meeting. This volume, printed in 1936 and again in 1945, has become a standard work in the religious education library.

In addition to her indefatigable authorship of lessons, a major contribution to religious education made by Jane was the preparation from 1916 to 1945 of the quarterly *First-day School Bulletin* (since 1942 *Religious Education Bulletin*). She wrote almost the entire content until the last five years when her lessened familiarity with the field caused her to invite perhaps 15 per cent of the material from others. Each number was four pages. Reading the *Bulletin* through as a whole, we find in it remarkable imagination, variety, and fertility of ideas. It presents original object lessons, games, puzzles, acrostics, enigmas, true and false tests, Bible quizzes. It suggests standards to test fitness of material, methods of conducting a class, devices for teaching. "Some teachers are born and not made, but most of our successful ones are self-made," the author remarks. Specific programs are given occasionally, particularly if they are ones originally worked out by a First-day school class, such as an experiment in writing present-day psalms, or a modern litany of praise, or a project of a whole school in the history of its Meeting, care of its property, or in social service.

Careful planning of the class work by teachers is repeatedly urged, and the constant keeping in mind of the essential purpose of the First-day school. "Spiritual growth cannot be attained by any magic formula. It comes more slowly than physical growth and never reaches a stopping place unless it is stunted or suffers injury. Like physical growth, it thrives by what it feeds upon. First-day school teachers are engaged in purveying nutriment."* At another time she points out:

> The purpose of religious education is not to solve special problems, but to develop people who will be able to solve difficult problems as they arise. The material used in classes is a tool to help the teacher's work of helping develop morally courageous, spiritually sensitive, and intellectually alert individuals. Such being the case, the subject matter of lesson texts is of less importance than the way it is used.†

Jane was prepared to give all the assistance she could to any teacher or school that consulted her. She has always been primarily an educator herself, and teaching teachers has been one her great abilities. But sometimes too much was asked of her. She cautions in the *Bulletin*, "Headquarters wishes to announce that it has no supply

---

* *First-day School Bulletin*, Vol. XXVIII, No. 1.

† *Ibid.*, Vol. XXVI, No. 2.

of teachers on hand either for sale, rent, or gratuitous distribution. . . . Every Friends' community should be developing teachers for home consumption."*

Again and again the emphasis is on worship. Prayer for children is helpfully discussed, and training for Quaker worship. "The theory of worship ought to be carefully taught in every First-day school. This may be accomplished either through explanation to the school as a whole, by class instruction, or by continued effort through the group interest of the younger children, conducted somewhat after the manner of a kindergarten morning circle. Such instruction should appeal to the intellect, the emotions, and the will. To the intellect so that we may understand what it means to lift up our hearts to God and why we Friends worship in silence; to the emotions so that we may feel the need and desire to enter into a state of worship; and to the will so that we will decide to try to use our opportunities for worship."† She adds:

> Schools ought to make more effort to impress upon classes that Jesus was a pioneer, a vigorous and fearless leader into the realm of new details and practices. A disproportionate amount of time is spent on birth stories and miracles‡ and not enough on the strength and power of a great leader whom we are challenged to follow.§

And when in worship and in life we have begun to try to follow him "we are likely to act as Jesus acted if we feel as he felt toward men."¶ In one of the last numbers that

* *Ibid.*, Vol. XXIII, No. 4.
† *Ibid.*, Vol. XI, No. 1.
‡ Verbal correction made by J. P. R.
§ *First-day School Bulletin*, Vol. XXV, No. 3.
¶ *Ibid.*, Vol. XVI, No. 2.

she wrote, Jane speaks again of the need of leadership by the teachers in bringing children to a reliance on God. "If we expect to teach children to believe in unseen realities, it is necessary that we ourselves should trust unseen powers."*

It is impossible to separate Jane's work for the Philadelphia committee from that done for the Conference, especially after the opening of the Bureau. The writing of lessons, the courses in teacher training, the counseling given to the schools, were done for Friends throughout the Conference. Philadelphia, however, especially developed activity in religious education, as it had by far the largest number of schools. Of approximately one hundred schools in the Conference in 1937, Philadelphia had about sixty-five, Baltimore and New York each about fifteen, and the smaller Yearly Meetings only two or three apiece. When the legacy from Emma R. Comly for the use of Philadelphia Yearly Meeting created the Comly Fund in 1935, a grant was made to provide study courses for teachers. Enrolled classes were arranged with a paid leader, and books were loaned from the Central Bureau library. The fund also helped the training work at Camp Keewadin and in these two ways benefited all the Conference teachers. In recent years under the direction of Amelia W. Swayne excellent work has been done in the Philadelphia area with a well-sustained program of local institutes.

Regular visiting of the schools was inaugurated in 1924, first by a committee of volunteers, whose expenses were paid by the First-day School Committee, and later by a part-time member of the Central Bureau staff. A good

* *Ibid.*, Vol. XXX, No. 1.

deal of effort has thus constantly gone into trying to bring the religious schools to some degree of efficiency, which, however, never remains constant because of the turnover in superintendents and teachers and the lack of overhead authority. Curricula have to be adapted to the widely differing conditions and schools have to be persuaded sometimes to do more work than they had hoped. Jane once advised:

> The subject matter used in First-day schools is important but is not the only thing which helps to make the success of a school. Teachers need not only to make a wise choice of subject matter, but to study the method and order in which it is presented from grade to grade. The central office has no self-acting material.*

The Religious Education Committee (thus renamed in 1941) now has struggled for sixty years to develop skills in transmitting religious teaching to children. Perhaps its aims have been most clearly defined in the *Bulletin* for First Month, 1936, in which the objectives were stated thus:

> 1. Religious education seeks to foster in growing persons a consciousness of God as a reality in human experience, a sense of personal relationship to Him, and the practice of communing with Him through worship (finding Him through Jesus' teaching and example, finding Him through the Inner Light); 2. religious education seeks to guide growing persons in the development of the highest moral character with the aim of applying the Christian motive in the making of all life choices; 3. religious education seeks to guide growing persons in finding God increasingly through service with and for men.

For thirty-one years Jane Rushmore sat on the Religious Education Committee. As she watched its work from almost the start to the present time, she finds that there have in fact been great advances. The Committee,

* *Ibid.*, Vol. I, No. 4.

now cooperating with a similar committee of Arch Street, has active subgroups working on curriculum, teacher-training, worship, home and family, and on high-school young people. With Amelia W. Swayne as chairman, it is one of the very effective arms of the Yearly Meeting.

In 1912, when her most active work for the First-day School Committee was just beginning, Jane was also appointed to Philadelphia's Philanthropic Committee. In 1892 the Committee on the Subject of Philanthropic Labor had been set up to bring into closer relationship the social interests of the Yearly Meeting. It included the formerly separate committees on Peace and Arbitration, Temperance and Tobacco, Improper Publications, Indian Affairs, and the Colored People. (The principal activity of the last of these committees was support of a few schools in the South for Negroes.) Shortly after Jane's appointment the reverse process of fragmentation was to start.

With the breaking out of World War I, Friends' always real concern for peace flared up into need for more action. It was felt that peace should be made the subject of work for a separate group. Dividing from the Philanthropic, the Emergency Peace Committee was set up in 1916 with an appropriation of $1500 and a deep concern to spread sentiment in favor of reducing if possible the already great conflict and preventing its further extension. It began a busy program of open-air meetings, automobile speaking tours, conferences, large public meetings held with the coöperation of Arch Street Friends, and similar plans. When in 1917 the American Friends Service Committee was formed, near the time that the United States entered the war, the Race Street Committee coöperated heartily with the over-all Friends' effort and changed its name to Committee on Peace and Emergency Service. By 1919 a paragraph in the report to the Yearly Meeting made this fruitful statement:

> We have held two sessions in conjunction with Arch Street Friends and have worked and taken counsel with them wherever possible. They are better organized than ourselves and have carried their work farther and more efficiently; but they have shown a cordial willingness to help us with their experience and to use every possible opportunity to join with us for common ends. We are glad to include in this public report the expression of our appreciation of their fellowship.

Thus begun, the coöperation progressively ripened until in the Yearly Meeting of 1933 a unification of the peace work of the two Yearly Meetings was proposed, and the two committees merged as the Peace Committee of Philadelphia and Vicinity, with an office at 304 Arch Street, Richard R. Wood as executive secretary, and two cochairmen, one from each Yearly Meeting.

Among those who took prominent part in this whole development was the first chairman of the Emergency Peace Committee, Jesse H. Holmes. Professor of philosophy and religion at Swarthmore College, he animated many of the concerns of the Philanthropic Committee, helped form the American Friends Service Committee, and was for years a member of its Peace Section. A valiant crusader for a number of causes, he unhesitatingly attacked the self-satisfied and the unthinking, and just as unreservedly accepted "the leadership of that Inner Light that would not let him be content or passive in a world torn by hatreds and bigotry."* Regarded as a prophet by some and as a firebrand by others, or both by the same person at different times, he in turn offended or inspired by his zealous,

---

* William W. Price, "Jesse H. Holmes," in *Quaker Torchbearers* (Philadelphia, 1943), p. 20.

unguarded speech. He used a characteristic title for one of his addresses, "Religion, a Spur or a Cushion?" There was no doubt which it was to him.

Friends' work for peace in the last half-century was appreciably advanced by the notable contribution of William I. and Hannah Clothier Hull, both untiring in the work of the Peace Committee. William Hull, professor of history and international relations at Swarthmore College, was an eminent writer of Quaker history, an uncompromising pacifist, and an early advocate of total, universal disarmament. He was sent by the American Friends Service Committee to Paris as observer and consultant while the Covenant of the League of Nations was being drafted. The Yearly Meeting asked him to attend both the Washington Disarmament Conference in 1922, and the Geneva General Disarmament Conference of 1932.* Hannah C. Hull worked prominently in the Women's International League for Peace and Freedom, side by side for many years with Lucy Biddle Lewis. Although peace was the most active interest of these Friends, they were deeply concerned in all the affairs of the Yearly Meeting, the General Conference, and the American Friends Service Committee, of which Hannah was for a number of years a vice-chairman.

While the formation of a joint Peace Committee was slowly maturing, a similar development was taking place in the section of the Philanthropic Committee which had been supporting the southern schools. Under the stimulation of Anne Biddle Stirling, Friends in this group formed an independent committee. In 1921 they asked the Yearly Meeting to set them off as the Committee on Interests of the Colored Race. They also absorbed such work for

* Richmond P. Miller, "William I. Hull," in *Quaker Torchbearers* (Philadelphia, 1943), pp. 21 ff.

Indians as was then being done, until that became independent again in a joint committee with Arch Street. Developing a growing fellowship between themselves and a similar Arch Street group, by 1930 the two groups had become a single Committee on Race Relations reporting to both Yearly Meetings, with coöperating chairmen, one from each side.

In 1912, when Jane Rushmore came to the Philanthropic Committee, it also had sections on prison reform, industrial conditions, and equal rights for women, a subject on which Quaker women naturally felt strongly because of the Society's traditional respect for the equivalent abilities of both sexes. Work for prisons and prisoners had a phase of greatly increased activity when Anna Wharton Morris and Louis N. Robinson were able to give it a good deal of time. When these two leaders had to withdraw, the work was largely suspended for a number of years until its recent revival under Leon T. Stern. The section on equal rights for women came to an end with the granting of national suffrage to women.

As a member of the Philanthropic Committee until 1924, Jane saw all these developments and welcomed them. Although she was no longer on the Committee when its further later detachments occurred, her position in the Central Bureau kept her familiar with its actions. The temperance section with very small funds had for years been able to do little but print leaflets—often very good ones—buy a few books, give some lectures, suggest some recommended study. In 1932 it also left the sheltering umbrella of the Philanthropic Committee, joined with Arch Street Friends, and with an enlarged budget took on a more productive aspect.

The remainder of the old Committee's subgroups reconsidered their position. The cycle was almost complete from independent work of the several interests to amalgamation and back to independence. It was clear that a new pattern was in order for those sections which had not already formed one. Since 1930 the idea of more modern social work had been growing. By 1936 the Philanthropic Committee was ready to propose to the Yearly Meeting a change in its name to Social Service, a reorganization, and the addition to the Central Bureau staff of a secretary for its activity. The Yearly Meeting approved, and Mary Hobson Jones came to the office in that summer. For the three and a half years she was with the Committee she visited widely among the Meetings, conducting study and discussion periods, directing community surveys, arranging visits to various institutions, and initiating a large October conference on social work. Under her and later under Richmond P. Miller this conference has been a successful annual event, bringing together two hundred or more persons: workers in social agencies of the whole Philadelphia area with appointed representatives of the Monthly Meetings. Richmond Miller since 1940 has given special attention to the interests of the Social Service Committee, though the main part of his time is devoted to field work for the Representative Committee.

In 1937 the Social Service Committee appointed some of its members to serve with the Social Order Committee of Arch Street for the study of certain economic problems. From this work there developed a joint group which by 1947 became completely merged under the Arch Street name of the Social Order Committee and with the usual arrangement of two chairmen. The field of this united Committee has been work camps and neighborhood improvement projects for young people under David S.

Richie as secretary, along with conferences on industrial and economic questions. Remaining within the jurisdiction of Race Street Yearly Meeting alone is the original Social Service Committee, dealing with, in 1951, penology, problems of aging Friends, displaced persons who have arrived in Philadelphia, and the annual conference of social workers.

Besides the continuous service over many years that Jane Rushmore gave to religious education and to philanthropic interests, there is a long list of her shorter terms in other fields. In 1909 the Yearly Meeting had inaugurated a plan of a General Nominating Committee and of four-year terms of appointment in most committees. With the increasing business of the annual sessions it was a great saving of time to deflect this important but slow operation from the Meeting itself. As soon as Jane started work in the Bureau it was obvious that her widening knowledge of the constituency made her so valuable that she was put on the Nominating Committee almost undeviatingly every other term (members of this committee cannot succeed themselves at once).

There were several occasions when minor or major revisions of the *Discipline* were made. Jane served on the committees appointed for the purpose. In the general revision of 1927, she wrote the section on the Scriptures and worked on business procedures. In 1924 she began a long succession of terms on the Budget Committee, which was instituted to replace the somewhat hit or miss, and thereby disproportioned, appropriations made from the floor during Yearly Meeting sessions. In this position Jane held an important post as the funds at the Yearly Meeting's disposition expanded. When the Budget Committee was changed into the Finance Committee in 1936,

Jane stayed with it for ten years longer. Parallel with all these services must be remembered her twenty-five or more years on the Central Committee of the General Conference.

No sooner was she released from the Philanthropic Committee in 1924 than she immediately moved to the Committee on Education and the Disposition of the Income of the Samuel Jeanes Fund. Here again she was in the area of one of her own primary interests.

As far back as when Jane was teaching at London Grove, the Committee on Education and Schools was disturbed over the state of the elementary schools scattered throughout the Yearly Meeting. The proposal was made that an outsider be asked to visit them and give suggestions. Because the London Grove School was growing larger by reason of excellent pedagogical methods, its principal was chosen to undertake the survey, and because London Grove closed a month earlier than many other schools, Jane had the time for visiting. She made an exhaustive report, with no reservations, which was helpful in directing the thinking of the Committee. Following her survey Ellen H. E. Price was appointed a full-time advisory officer, a position she held for several years.

Meanwhile in 1895 an extraordinary occurrence had begun to benefit the Friends' schools. A modest Quaker family in Philadelphia named Jeanes that had accumulated a good deal of money found itself growing old without descendants. Two brothers and two sisters, all unmarried, made each other their heirs. During the early nineties three of them died, their several estates concentrating in the hands of the one remaining sister, Anna T. Jeanes. Obviously some serious decisions must be made by this no longer young woman. She did not consult anyone so far as is known, but she gave careful thought to practical uses for the money.

The Yearly Meeting of 1895 had reconvened after one of its noon recesses. Someone later recalled that a colored man had previously slipped in and gone out again. Charles Jenkins later wrote to Jane Rushmore,

> At the business session of Men's Yearly Meeting on Fifth Month 13th, 1895, when the meeting gathered in the afternoon an envelope, addressed to the meeting, was found on the clerk's desk. . . . The clerk [Emmor Roberts] opened it and announced there was a communication addressed to the meeting which should be read at this time. It was from Anna T. Jeanes with a check enclosed for $200,000 "donated from the estate of Samuel Jeanes" to be applied to educational purposes.

This was the first of the benefactions of Anna Jeanes given into the care of the Yearly Meeting, which, together with her bequests by will, ultimately reached nearly $3,000,000.

> I well remember [Charles Jenkins continues] the sensation in the Yearly Meeting when the clerk produced the first letter and made the announcement that $200,000 had been given to the Yearly Meeting. One other donation from her came in the same spectacular way, but I cannot recall how the others were presented to the meeting. We got to expecting one every year, and were a little disappointed if one did not turn up.

The story of one of the other funds Jane heard from Edmund Webster, treasurer of the Yearly Meeting. Soon after the first gift was made, the Committee on Education had used some of the income as a loan to students. When Anna Jeanes learned of this she betook herself at once to the treasurer. "That is not what Brother Samuel would have approved," she protested emphatically. "The money must be returned to the fund." Edmund Webster regretted very much that the Committee had erred. No more money would be used in this way and what had been loaned would be replaced. It would mean that such and such students at such and such schools would have their education stopped, he continued, giving details. Anna Jeanes took out her checkbook and pen. "This is Sister Mary's money. I do not think she would object to loaning money to young people who need help." She handed him a check for $30,000, which became the Mary Jeanes Fund, used as a loan fund for student aid.*

Later the Committee on Education (it had adopted the long descriptive title in 1897 after the first Jeanes gift, but shortened it in 1925) had a legacy from Anne P. Townsend to provide outright gifts to students who wished to be fitted for making a living outside of teaching. The distribution of the income of these gifts was an important part of the Committee's work. Its other major task was its advisory care over the Friends' schools in the Yearly Meeting, exclusive of George School which was governed by its own Yearly Meeting committee.

In the eighteenth century almost as soon as a meeting house was built, a schoolhouse was erected beside it. At one time there were, according to Howard Brinton,† at least sixty Friends' schools in Pennsylvania within fifty miles of Philadelphia, and perhaps thirty in New Jersey. As the public education system increased the number of schools and the money available to them, Quaker schools decreased, until in 1911 there were only twenty-three in Race Street Yearly Meeting. Yet the concern for a rightly guided education persisted strongly among Friends. The Education Committee with the assistance of the Samuel Jeanes Fund began improving the quality of schools that

---

* See account by Jane P. Rushmore, "Anna T. Jeanes," in *Quaker Torchbearers* (Philadelphia, 1943), pp. 164 ff.

† *Friend*, Sixth month 28, 1951, p. 405.

were lagging behind rising standards. As secretary of the Committee (the word supervisor was not used because the position carried no authority), Ida Palmer Stabler, a trained normal-school instructor, visited and advised with the schools for a number of years. In 1924 Emma B. Wallace became the officer of the Education Committee, and for twenty-six years thereafter she was devoted and untiring in her care and encouragement of the schools. During that period a few more of them closed, as Friends left their neighborhood or for other reasons. On the other hand, in recent years some new ones have been started, old ones reopened, enrollments have increased, and additions to buildings have been made.

One of Emma Wallace's persistent ambitions was to see a united Quaker educational effort. In this field there was no conflict between the principles of the two branches of Friends; the schools were conducted in the same way for the same purposes. A beginning was made through social contacts of the principals of high schools. Later the principals of the elementary schools organized. The two Yearly Meeting committees for several years occasionally conferred. The secretaries started visiting the schools together. At last in 1949 a single committee was inaugurated, whose members are appointed by the two Yearly Meetings. One treasurer manages all the funds which are jointly used. The twenty-two schools now under the able direction of Isabel F. Randolph with their 4665 students are the most conspicuous expression of united Philadelphia Quakerism.

Jane Rushmore took a far more direct part in this development than being merely an interested member of the Education Committee. Such indeed she was, always making valuable and progressive contributions to discussion. But in addition to that, her concern with the philosophy, attitudes, and sense of direction of local committees and teachers was expressed, as has been stated earlier, through her constant writing in the *Courier,* a four-page quarterly, which from its beginning in 1937 through June 1952 she wrote entirely by herself. In this leaflet she reiterated what the basis of a Friends' school should be and why it was a religious concern. No doubt her years at London Grove and Kennett Square did much to sharpen and clarify her own conception of the function of Quaker schools in a world where public schools are constantly improving. There are still those who argue that private schools are only for snobs or incompetents. "A genuine Friends' school," Jane wrote, "is an important factor in carrying forward into the coming generation of citizens the ideals of life which we cherish. . . . We are trying to develop future men and women whose way of life will uphold our principles of sincerity and simplicity and democracy."* But the public schools teach democracy better, say the doubters, because so many different kinds of children meet there. The Friends' schools admit this great variety of background as a real value. To take its place they try to supply concerned teachers, who, working experimentally with small classes, can carry the idea even further, to the acceptance of responsibility which is inherent in a country which values its freedom. Jane wrote "Perhaps the most important function of a truly liberal education is to stimulate genuine thinking about important human relationships."† Later she said:

* *Courier,* September 1950.
† *Ibid.,* May 1937.

UNDER QUAKER APPOINTMENT

Some members of the human family are incompetent, evil-minded and ill-disposed, but the line of demarcation between them and the competent, honorable and diligent members of society is neither the color line nor a barrier of wealth and social position. An effort to understand people, to know why they are as they are, and a concern to change them for the better, are fundamental bases to helpful human relationships.*

A new and important attempt to interpret Quaker education in just this way had been begun with the opening of George School. Antedating any of the Jeanes gifts had been the decision of John M. George to leave the bulk of his estate to Philadelphia Yearly Meeting for the building and endowing of a boarding school for boys and girls. When the bequest of some $700,000 arrived, the Yearly Meeting at once, in 1888, set up a committee of sixty-eight Friends to select a site and study the possible scope and character of the future school. Deborah Stubbs, in whose home Jane was then living, was appointed to the original committee, serving on it about ten years. While the interest of all Friends was greatly attracted by this major undertaking of the Yearly Meeting, Jane Rushmore was especially concerned as she and the Stubbs family talked over the project in London Grove on Deborah's return from her long meetings. Jane was never put on this Committee, but from the start she knew a number who were important members, such as Robert L. Pyle, Alfred D. Sharples of West Chester, and William Wade Griscom of Woodbury, N. J., the first clerk. Not until 1892 was the location near Newtown, Pa., finally purchased. The Main Building opened for its first academic year in the fall of 1893.

On August 18 of that year a great picnic had been held on the grounds to afford a view of the partly finished build-

* *Ibid.*, December 1947.

ing and the campus. A beautiful day encouraged attendance; Friends arrived by train, carriages, wagons, and stagecoaches. They swarmed among the plasterers, bricklayers, carpenters, and steam fitters; they climbed to the roof to enjoy the long vista of rolling country. By afternoon when the program of speeches began, the crowd was estimated to number between two thousand and twenty-five hundred. Many noted the especially fine address given by Joseph S. Walton.

When the school opened George L. Maris, the principal, the small faculty, two of whom were Jesse H. Holmes and George H. Nutt, and the first 130 boarding students had all the standards, policies, and traditions to set. It was a big adventure. The school and the committee learned together the business of conducting a boarding school for the Yearly Meeting.

After eight years George Maris resigned. The George School Committee recalled the good speech of Joseph Walton at the picnic. He had continued for a time as superintendent of the Chester County schools, resigned to become instructor in history for two years at West Chester State Normal School, and in 1898 had been made principal of Friends' Central School in Philadelphia. The Committee appointed Joseph S. Walton to the George School principalship. With him came, in that autumn of 1901, his sister, Deborah F. Stubbs. Dr. Stubbs had died; his widow needed further resources for the education of her children. She resigned from the Committee and accepted appointment to the position of "matron." All of her successors have been called "dean," but even that title scarcely describes the place Deborah Stubbs occupied. She was in fact, as the history of the school relates,* actually

* *History of George School, 1893-1943.* Published by George School Alumni Association, 1943.

a coprincipal, giving the greatest encouragement and support to her brother, sharing with him all considerations of important policy and practice. She continued at the school for several years after his untimely death in 1912, maintaining her great influence on the students by her humor, sympathy, and religious power, and again helping with a firm hand the new principal, her nephew George A. Walton, son of his predecessor.

For the thirty-six years of his principalship, Jane Rushmore watched the progress of the school almost as closely as in the early days of experiment by his father and Deborah Stubbs. George Walton's organizing ability, his gift as a speaker, and his success as a teacher stimulated the growth of the student body and the constant increase of plant and facilities. Under him also the original conception of the Friendly character of the school was continued and strengthened. Students attended meeting for worship at Newtown or at school. In the first years religious instruction was given in Newtown First-day School and courses in the Bible were part of the regular curriculum. As early as 1906 classes in religious education were taught by Eleanor Wood (Whitman) and later, in 1908, by George Walton. Ultimately the course was enlarged until it was placed under a full-time director of religious interests.

The devotion to Quaker ideals of the faculty, whether members of the Society of Friends or not (a number have become Friends through their association with the school), has well satisfied the Yearly Meeting that the young people are being trained in a way that puts conscience and the needs of humanity first.

Perhaps the philosophy of Quaker education is as succinctly stated as can be found anywhere in a comment of Jane's in the *Courier* of June 1951, when she says: "We think a man is educated not when he is replete with knowledge of many things, but when he has the full use of all his potential possibilities and knows how to put these powers into effective and altruistic action." Emphasis on altruistic action, on the concern to change people for the better, on a sense of moral values, is, Friends hope, a distinctive mark of all their schools, not only the small circuit of those under the Education Committee but those within the orbit of all the other Yearly Meetings.

Indeed, some twenty years ago a movement to unite the interests of Quaker schools everywhere in America was initiated by Arch Street. J. Henry Bartlett had been in England, where he became interested in a council on education which Friends had established there. On his return he began working out a similar plan. After a brief trial of it the Friends General Conference and Five Years Meeting Education Board were invited to join. This in 1932 became the Friends Council on Education, in which New York and Baltimore (General Conference) Yearly Meetings as well as Philadelphia joined, and also the Education Board of the Five Years Meeting. All of these groups appoint a definite number of representatives; the principals of the high schools, and more recently the principals of all Friends' schools, belong to it, plus the executive secretary of the Philadelphia Committee on Education. It has an office at 20 South Twelfth Street and an office secretary, but at present no executive director. Its purpose is to unify so far as is beneficial all Friends' education in America through conferring together and working toward the same aims and purposes. Complete unity has not been achieved, but increasing acquaintance and coöperation have been very useful. Jane Rushmore was an active member of the Council, representing Race Street, from its beginning until the early fifties. Since then she has been an honorary member.

UNDER QUAKER APPOINTMENT

Of the range of work carried on throughout Philadelphia Yearly Meeting there has been little indeed with which Jane Rushmore was not intimately acquainted. She spent thirty-one years as a member of the First-day School Committee helping to raise standards in religious education. Her briefer part in the Philanthropic Committee saw it begin more vital and energetic accomplishment as one interest after another separated out to become independent and then found helpful coöperation with Arch Street Friends. Her life-long devotion to education found expression in the Quaker committee from 1924 to the present time. With the additional time she gave to budgets, to nominating committees, to many comparatively short-term assignments, and to Quarterly and Monthly Meeting affairs, she personally covered a large section of Quaker activity, and her knowledge embraced nearly the whole gamut. Even when she gave up actual membership on committees, or even with those she did not serve, her central position at the Bureau and her wide acquaintance kept her up to date on current progress. She became a compendium of knowledge on Quaker business, unfailingly available to any who needed to consult her. She was untiringly willing to contribute her time and strength to any project or on any errand the Meetings asked. It might be in the line of her regular duties at the Bureau, or for whatever committee she was on, or entirely outside of either. No call found her unready. Every day appeared to be given practically in its entirety to the Society of Friends, its secular and religious interests, which to her mind were the same. Yet all was done as a matter of course—a quite normal offering, which, as Paul said long ago to a little church in Rome, is your reasonable service. Nor is the tale of it yet complete.

CHAPTER IX

From the Clerk's Table

As the Society of Friends is organized, its central authority is vested in the Yearly Meeting. Between this body and the Monthly Meeting, the local unit in which individual memberships reside, stands the Quarterly Meeting gathering together Monthly Meetings of a convenient geographical area, sitting once every three months, or quarter, reporting directly to the Yearly Meeting on behalf of its component groups, but having few functions of initiation. The Yearly Meeting is thus the apex of the system of subordinate bodies. To a very real degree it is both a centripetal and a centrifugal force, receiving and dispensing the social and spiritual powers of its members as Friends are sent from local Meetings to pour their energy into the work of the Yearly Meeting committees, and as that Meeting in turn offers its services in many forms to its local groups, or takes its place in still larger units such as Friends General Conference.

For generations Friends have felt attendance at the annual sessions a serious duty. Members used to gather from long distances. They arranged to leave their homes and usually stayed with local families for the duration of "Yearly Meeting Week." They expected to attend every session. The meeting was an august and dignified body where each Friend might be heard. Its decisions were not arrived at until any who disagreed with the proposal were either convinced or willing not to press their side further in view of the feelings of others. If such agreement was not achieved, the matter was not acted on at all, but "laid over" until Friends were "in unity." The men and women sat separately, as they had from the beginning. In the seventeenth century this custom had been a signal recognition of the equal status of women. By the end of the nineteenth it was beginning to be recognized as unnecessarily cumbersome.

When Jane Rushmore became a resident of Pennsylvania in 1884, the rule for holding Philadelphia Yearly Meeting was that the business sessions should begin on the "first Second-day following the second First-day in the Fifth month." They usually adjourned the afternoon of the following Sixth-day (Friday). Jane at first did not attend Yearly Meeting since London Grove School closed before this time and there was no reason for her not going straight home at the end of the school term. Several years later when she did stay, the clerk of the Women's Meeting was Margaretta Walton, that Friend whom she had known for many summers at Potter Hollow and who had recommended her for the position at London Grove.

Jane gives the following account of her impressions:

> When I first remember Philadelphia Yearly Meeting before 1890 Margaretta Walton and Matilda Garrigues sat at the table. Both were notably impressive persons. Margaretta, clad in the costume which Friends traditionally wore but which was disappearing, was a handsome woman whose highly spiritual quality seemed to extend over the whole meeting. I often marveled that this could be the same warmly human person that I knew, who loved bright colors, was keenly interested in the welfare of people, and understood a humorous situation. Matilda, the assistant clerk, was a memorable reader.
>
> Everything was deeply serious. The business was of a routine character, interspersed with vocal messages from concerned Friends. The minutes were never outlined in advance. Every sentence was written from the beginning during the sessions by the clerk, who was, as always, both chairman and secretary, and the pauses thus necessitated were opportunities for extended preaching. Worldly

FROM THE CLERK'S TABLE

matters like finance must be barely touched upon, the only allusion to them being approval of necessary expenses.

Everything was slow, new subjects were rarely introduced. All epistles received from other Yearly Meetings were read in their entirety. Formal, often uninforming, replies to all the Queries were read and summarized. It all impressed me, but I thought it dull and not headed anywhere: What could be done with a summary of summaries from Quarterly Meetings? A Committee on Exercises was always appointed to gather and record the substance of the vocal ministry or discussion during the week. It was astonishing how much better the committee's report sounded than the original speaking.

Sarah Griscom succeeded Margaretta Walton as clerk in 1893. A small woman, wearing a modified "plain dress," she held the meeting in firm control, permitting no laughter to mar the austere dignity of the sessions. She was a despot, Jane says, but no one knew it, for she was just and able. For twenty-nine years she carried the rather heavy responsibilities of the clerkship, at first with Matilda Garrigues beside her as assistant.

All three of the presiders had a little hidden fun at their table, in spite of outward solemnity. Once when Matilda Garrigues asked Margaretta Walton why the next piece of business was not taken up, the clerk whispered back, "If thee'll just wait a minute, I think I'm going to preach." Part of the assistant's work was to integrate the exercises into the minutes, which were read aloud the following morning. She did this by making symbols to indicate references to inserted pages. But Matilda did not use letters or numbers or asterisks. She made tiny drawings of leaves or other figures. More than once Sarah Griscom's lips twitched as she followed directions via a pig with a curly tail or a dog with a cocked ear.

After the retirement of Matilda Garrigues, Sarah Griscom had a succession of assistants, a new one almost every year. As the Yearly Meeting's business increased and home duties became more demanding, Sarah Griscom felt that she needed assistance from someone who knew the Meeting's concerns. In fact she wanted Jane Rushmore, who had now been at the Central Bureau for seven years. When the official representatives, who nominate the clerks, learned of Sarah Griscom's desire, one of them, Caroline S. Jackson, asked Jane if she would be willing to serve. Jane said, "Will the Yearly Meeting approve of an assistant at the desk who is paid by the Yearly Meeting for work in the Bureau?" Caroline Jackson replied, "I never thought of that." Then after a moment's pause, she added, "I think that does not matter. We think of thee as a concerned Friend, not as an employee."

The appointment was made and continued until Sarah Griscom asked to retire four years later, in 1922. Then Jane Rushmore became the clerk of the Women's Yearly Meeting. In all Jane conducted the business from the clerk's table for more than five years. During that time an outstanding change occurred.

In 1921 it had been proposed that men and women hold one of their sessions together. Many of the subordinate meetings had by now given up separate business meetings of men and women, and this crack in the tradition of 240 years, while ominous to some, to others seemed a hint of progress. One joint session was held. In 1922, Jane's first year as clerk, joint sessions were held on two days, and the next year on three. Then in 1924, with three successful experiments behind them, Friends were prepared to take the momentous step of permanent joint sessions. Men and women were convened separately on Second-day morning for each group to take the proper action of formally adjourning into a single body, and then reconvening into the

FROM THE CLERK'S TABLE

united group. Philadelphia was far behind the other General Conference Yearly Meetings in this move. New York had met jointly for twenty-five years or more, and the others far longer. The most startling aspect of the metamorphosis in Philadelphia was in the selection of the first clerk for the combined Meeting. The delegates proposed a woman. As scarcely needs to be said that woman was Jane P. Rushmore. She herself was greatly surprised.

After two years Jane was succeeded as clerk by George A. Walton, then principal of George School. When he was absent on a trip to England in 1929, she was again called to serve for the year, and she also filled in for the remaining sessions of 1932 after George Walton became ill on the opening day. Jane Rushmore therefore served for two years as clerk of the Women's Meeting, three years for the combined Yearly Meeting, and several additional days. All of the clerks since that time have been men.

Jane recalls a few of the prominent figures of thirty years ago.

At the time that I assumed the clerkship, among the women Friends most frequently taking part in the business was Sarah B. Flitcraft of Chester, tall and fine looking. She spoke clearly with a firm belief that conservatism was synonymous with Quakerism. Mary R. Livezey, of Norristown, generally advanced the same point of view, though she was a little more open to considering present-day interests. Caroline S. Jackson carried a large measure of responsible service, a woman with convictions and the courage to stand by them. Among those representing a desire for a more forward-looking Society was Elizabeth Lloyd. She was always urging speakers to come to the front of the meeting so they could be heard. She once said, "There are only about thirty of us who ever contribute anything vocally to the Yearly Meeting, and the front seats will accommodate them all." I had considerable amusement over trying to find out who the thirty persons were who conducted the business of the Yearly Meeting.

Lucy Biddle Lewis was then at the peak of her great abilities.

She was very stirring [continues Jane], spoke often, always as an advocate of progress. She was thought to be very radical, but she was considerate of the views of others. There was quite a time over the proposal to have the clerks named by the General Nominating Committee instead of by the representatives to the Yearly Meeting. Eight important Friends in the front gallery opposed the change; the body of the meeting favored it. After I, as clerk, suggested postponing action for a year, saying that the objectors had borne the concerns of the Meeting for many years and that it was Friends' way to wait for unity, Lucy Lewis, herself anxious for the change, at once said, "Of course, we'll wait a year and then discuss it again." By that time all were ready for the new plan. Lucy Lewis was usually supported by her close friend, Hannah Clothier Hull, whose gentle manner persuasively urged Friends to use their opportunities to exert a wider influence.

In the youths' gallery* directly facing the clerk, I recall three sisters, always on hand, who rarely spoke in the sessions of Yearly Meeting but were powers in committee work and in gathering up the proceedings, Anna Canby Janney, Lucy Smyth Cooper, and Frances Canby Chambers. In general the Women's Meeting had unity without uniformity. It was more progressive than the Men's, and under much better control. The philanthropic reports found the Women's Meeting more receptive, and new ideas were more likely to be approved.

Among the men Friends whom Jane knew best, she mentions especially Alfred Moore, a strong personality, clerk of the Representative Committee for a long time, and first president of the Incorporated Trustees.

He did all the legal work without pay for the Trustees. He was not an obstructionist though he wished to see that all proceedings were very regular. He was upheld in this view by Harrison Streeter, also a power in the Trustees, though both were willing to move out

---

* The old name for the second-floor balcony around the sides and back of the meeting house, as distinguished from the ministers' gallery raised a few steps above the main floor, facing the room.

of the past to meet the needs of the present provided all changes were made in a regular manner. Edmund Webster, treasurer of the Yearly Meeting for many years, served on almost every committee concerned with education. He was a member of the Swarthmore College Board, of the George School Committee, of the Friends' Central School Committee, and of the Yearly Meeting's Committee on Education. He generally said nothing if he thought things were going right, but quietly put a stop to movements which he believed were unsound. William P. Bancroft, of Wilmington, long chairman of the George School Committee, was very quiet also but knew how to get things done. He originated the plan for the General Nominating Committee, adopted in 1909. His wife, Emma C. Bancroft, was greatly interested in young people, helping many to advance their education though never letting them know where the help came from. Both were generous of their large resources in unostentatious ways. William Bancroft once had occasion to meet a steerage passenger arriving in New York. It was necessary for someone to vouch financially for such newcomers. "The inspector asked what my income was. I told him as nearly as I could. I do not think he believed me."

The government agent did not know the rigorous honesty of this plainly dressed man. He made large benefactions to Wilmington Friends School, George School, and Swarthmore College, besides innumerable donations which were successfully concealed.

In 1925, during Jane's clerkship, unrest about the *Book of Discipline* culminated in a proposal to rewrite the book, which had been amended many times. A large committee on revision was charged also with consulting the other five Hicksite Yearly Meetings with a view to adopting a discipline which would represent all Hicksite Friends. After two years of diligent effort the committee made a report which was approved at the Yearly Meeting. Baltimore, Genesee, Indiana, and Illinois adopted the same book with minor changes, since the ones they were using were all rather out of date. New York had, however, recently carried through a satisfactory revision of its own and preferred to retain that.

As accepted by Philadelphia, the new *Discipline* integrated the several Committees on Ministry and Counsel (the name adopted at this time in place of the former Ministers and Elders) more closely into the general structure. The way was thus prepared for making, a few years later, their annual "Select Meeting" on the day before the commencement of Yearly Meeting an open one. Still later the gathering became a regular session of the Yearly Meeting itself. Formal recommendation of ministers was abolished. This move was vigorously opposed by some Friends, but actually the practice had been largely given up for the past ten years. Many Meetings believed it undemocratic to specify some members as approved ministers, while others, less gifted perhaps but equally valued, were not so distinguished. The Representative Committee was redistricted, proportioning the number of members to the size of the Quarterly Meeting they represented and adding sixteen persons chosen at large. This altered significantly the character of the Committee, making it more representative of the Yearly Meeting.

The whole matter of the place occupied by the *Book of Discipline* in the Society of Friends is pointed up by the comparative ease with which these changes were made.

> A book of discipline is necessary to make our testimonies clear and to insure the orderly transaction of business [Jane wrote]. The book is not considered sacred, but is a serious exposition with which members should be in substantial agreement.
>
> The membership of a society without a creed must hold certain important testimonies in common . . . in order to provide the necessary coherence to be called a distinctive Religious Society. Our adherence to a central truth expressed as "the Inner Light," our democracy of worship and ministry, mark us as decidedly different from other Christian sects, though we hold many essential Christian testimonies in common with them. . . . A society that hopes to

maintain vigor and influence must rely upon the constant practical application of these testimonies in the lives of its members. A consistent opposition to war, intemperance, gambling, race prejudice and slavery of any kind is expected of every concerned Friend. We do not drop members who do not fully support the affirmations of the Discipline on all of these subjects, if they are in general sympathy with our profession and methods, but we hope always they will see the light and strengthen our testimonies.

In regard to making changes, Jane continues,

> We have fortunately emerged from the period when we felt that it was desecration to change the language and structure of the book in order to adapt it better to existing needs. . . . In general it is a sound principle that changes should not be made merely for the sake of change or experiment, but should never be delayed when it is clear that revised or additional statements will help the life of the Society.*

Jane Rushmore was, as we have seen, a member of the committee that carried through the general revision completed in 1927, though she was not clerk of the Yearly Meeting when the new form was adopted.

During the years that she presided changes had taken place. The very serious mien of the gathering was lightened, for Jane had a tendency to present matters in a way which was found amusing and she felt that the older restraint was unnecessary. She made the business move faster by having a part of the minutes written up ahead. She explains,

> It is the duty of the clerk to lay the proposition clearly before the Meeting and be sure that it is understood before any action is taken. The clerk knows what the business is beforehand. Since the statement of the case and the decision are all that are put in the minutes, the proposal can be transcribed in advance. Then the Meeting expresses itself, the clerk gathers the weight of opinion and writes the decision into the minute which can be approved on the spot.

---

* Jane P. Rushmore, *Testimonies and Practice of the Society of Friends* (Philadelphia, 1945), pp. 83, 84, 86.

The fear that the sessions would be unwieldy in size when the Men's and Women's Meetings were joined has not been realized. Recent decades find the attendance much smaller than in the earlier days which saw sometimes a thousand women in Race Street Meeting House with possibly four hundred men in the Cherry Street end of the building. But Jane is not at all disheartened by the reduction in numbers. Many more women, as well as men, are in commercial or industrial life, unable to command their own time as could farmers of a former day and housewives with servants. On the other hand, Jane points out, the number of persons carrying committee responsibility has greatly multiplied, so that fully as many people, or more, take part in Yearly Meeting activities and the work is more important and more effective.

CHAPTER X

Under Weighty Appointment

The Yearly Meeting sits for one week of the year. For the rest of the time the continuing body is not an executive board, but a much larger assembly. In London it holds the name given it in Quakerism's first decades of constant persecution, the "Meeting for Sufferings." Race Street calls it the Representative Committee. Originally it was composed of four representatives from each Quarterly and Half-Yearly Meeting, making it a group of forty-four, divided, but not always evenly, between men and women. In 1927 the new *Discipline* changed the proportions from the Quarters and enlarged the number. The status of this body is entirely different from that of the committees which carry out the specific testimonies and concerns of the Meeting such as religious education, peace, race relations, education, or George School. Since the Representative Committee is the Yearly Meeting when the latter is not in session, it has all the powers of the larger conclave except two, specifically withheld: namely, to change the *Discipline* and to impose taxes.

Curiously, the Men's Meeting over a period of years saw no particular value in having its clerk a member of the Committee, so that he assumed his important duties for Yearly Meeting Week without knowing what had gone on in the interim body. The women, however, saw to it that their presiding officer was always on the Representative Committee though not in an ex-officio capacity. Jane Rushmore was appointed to it in 1921, the year before she assumed clerkship of the Women's Meeting, and she remained a member until 1948.

UNDER QUAKER APPOINTMENT

When she first knew anything of the Committee's functioning, it transacted very little business; it was afraid of trespassing on the prerogatives of the Yearly Meeting and did only what it was instructed to carry out. It advised local Meetings on questions of property, acted on their requests for appropriations from the Samuel Jeanes Fund to repair their meeting houses, took care of the records in the fireproof room, and arranged the program for Yearly Meeting. It had a subcommittee, not very active, on "Increasing Interest among Our Members." Its two sessions a year, outside of the organization meeting, were ample for the business that came before it.

In the 1920's a change began taking place. Jane's experience as Yearly Meeting clerk led her to propose that certain routine matters be taken over by the Representative Committee and the Yearly Meeting's time be used for more valuable considerations. One matter transferred was the approval of names submitted by the General Nominating Committee. As the number of committees increased, the reading of the list of all appointees in the Yearly Meeting for its sanction was time-consuming, uninteresting, and was gone through with as fast as possible. The Representative Committee now gives careful attention to each name and takes final action.

On completing her fourth successive year as clerk of the Yearly Meeting in the spring of 1926, Jane was asked to assume the same responsible position of clerkship for the Representative Committee in 1927. Here for nineteen years she was in the most strategic place she ever occupied. She says now that whatever contribution she may have offered to the Society of Friends was made more largely through this avenue than any other. How much the reactivating of the Representative Committee was due to her initiative and how much to her practical encouragement of the proposals of others cannot be determined. The interesting point is how greatly the functions of the Committee increased and developed in these two decades. The revision of the *Discipline* in 1927 placed the Representative Committee in a position of leadership, and in Jane Rushmore it had a leader ready to go forward.

An important beginning was made at once with the appointment of a subcommittee on field work to visit Meetings and make a closer connection between them and the Yearly Meeting. The volunteer visitors were definitely not sent as a preaching mission. They were indeed, at the start, chosen from among those who did not speak in meetings for worship. They took their lunch with them, so as not to be a tax on local hospitality, and they conferred with the resident Friends about their problems. For instance, the difference in function between the Committee on Ministry and Counsel (to foster spiritual life) and the Overseers (to exercise pastoral care) was not always clearly understood. An effort was made to point out the important distinction between the two. "A few small Meetings." Jane wrote, "appoint but one group and assign to it all the duties usually carried by the two. This may be desirable when the membership is so small that all responsibilities must be carried by the same people. Its danger is that the development of interest in the practice of worship will be crowded out by the kind of material concerns which are easier to handle."*

While in 1926 four visits had been made to local Meetings, forty-five were made the next year, and more than eighty in 1934. Besides arranging these local visits, the field committee held for a number of years good field conferences, each embracing several Meetings, until at last it became clear that there was too much organization

* *Messenger*, Twelfth month, 1940.

and so the conferences were dropped. This subcommittee was soon the right arm of the Representative Committee. Richmond P. Miller became its secretary in 1940, dividing his time with the work of the Social Service Committee.

The work of the subcommittee on printing and publication was greatly expanded. In 1928 Jane proposed issuing a letter to the constituent local Meetings to keep the membership informed of Yearly Meeting activities. Called the *Messenger,* it was written by Jane herself until 1949, when Richmond Miller took it over. This small, four-page sheet appearing six times a year carried brief discourses or epigrammatic paragraphs on Quaker testimonies, principles, and affairs, with comments on items of current interest. The topics were appropriate to the general membership rather than to those directly connected with religious or secular education as in the *First-day School Bulletin* and the *Courier,* both of which Jane was concurrently writing. The purpose of the *Messenger* was not to be a news bulletin, or a column of "personals," but to keep clear the faith of Friends and the manner of its working out in practice.

As has been said, the publication of two books of readings, *The Higher Life* and *Founding a Home,* was authorized by the Representative Committee, as well as the annual printing of the *Calendar* and the less frequent issue of the *Book of Meetings,* although the Central Bureau took all the burden of compiling and editing them. A program of leaflets dealing with the basic principles of Friends was undertaken, one or two being published each year. When statements on the issues of the day are printed in the name of the Society, these must also have the approval of the Representative Committee and be published by it, no matter where initiated.

UNDER WEIGHTY APPOINTMENT

Overseers were often besought by young people for special information about marriages. If two non-Friends wanted to use Friends' ceremony, would that be legal? Could Friends use their form of marriage in states where there were no Friends? Such questions led to the collecting, through the facilities of the Central Bureau, of information on marriage laws in all the states where members of Race Street Yearly Meeting live, a greatly appreciated service.

During World War I the question of Friends' stand in opposition to all war and a statement in regard to it led to the inauguration of occasional joint conferences with the Arch Street Representative Meeting. Because of the difficulties created for Friends by World War II, the Representative Committee appointed an advisory committee to confer with men of draft age; it also devised plans to share in the financing of conscientious-objector camps through Civilian Public Service, a body set up by the American Friends Service Committee in coöperation with the Mennonites and Church of the Brethren.

The Representative Committee takes care of all arrangements for Yearly Meeting, even supplying some diversion. "When Charles and Marie Jenkins returned from a visit to London Yearly Meeting in 1928," Jane relates, "Charles, then a member of the Representative Committee, so impressed us with the socializing effect of tea drinking that we appointed a committee to serve tea each afternoon at the close of the business session." With the date of the Yearly Meeting moved since 1933 to March, this pleasant custom has proved an excellent replacement for the lively social hours previously enjoyed in the yard in the bright May weather.

The wider outlook of Quakerism after 1920 called for

frequent appointment of delegates to various convocations and acceptance of reports upon their return. Now all dealings with the American Friends Service Committee, the American Friends Fellowship Council, the Friends Committee on National Legislation, and other inclusive bodies go through the Representative Committee.

In the Yearly Meeting of 1930 the question was raised of having a field worker for the Philanthropic Committee. The discussion led to the conducting of an extensive survey directed by the Representative Committee to learn the needs and desires of local Meetings and their attitude toward increased financial outlay if a social service secretary was wanted. A questionnaire was sent by the Central Bureau and special visitors were appointed to confer with the Meetings, helping them to study their own problems before their answers were sent in. The questions embraced a wide field: the attendance and the quality of the meetings for worship, the conduct of business meetings, the condition of First-day schools, the strength of the Meetings' social concerns, and their financial status.

The visitors made some interesting discoveries that never would have been apparent if formal written answers had been the only basis of reporting. All Meetings avowed great interest in education, but in several cases the members who advocated increases in the budget to benefit the school were defeated. "Are you concerned about Indians?" the visitor would inquire. "Oh, yes." "What are you doing for them?" "Oh, well, Friends have always been interested in Indians." All announced that their greatest tie was to the meeting for worship. Yet in about half the localities the best attendance was in the First-day school. When a number of Meetings refused to report their budgets, persuasion had to be used. One was shown that its figures would prove to the Yearly Meeting that it had been unduly assessed, another that it would have more appreciation and credit if others knew how much it was doing for the Yearly Meeting. One, when asked if the quota assigned was a burden, said it was. Then it was disclosed that this Meeting held a small endowment and the membership made no contributions at all. Nevertheless, it felt the quota a burden because it did not make use of the helpful material and advice which the Yearly Meeting offered. Jane visited on this mission a number of Meetings, finding herself assigned to all the troublesome ones.

The outcome was a considerable clarification of the functioning and the financial state of the Yearly Meeting, although it was six years before the Philanthropic Committee was able to appoint a field worker. The Meetings as such were generally not dealing with social conditions except through the Yearly Meeting committees. Many members were active for local betterment in projects often originated and wholly or largely managed by Friends, but these undertakings were not a Meeting responsibility. Even temperance (prohibition was then a lively political issue) and race relations, both expressing testimonies long cherished by Friends, were much neglected. After calling on the membership to exert itself as vigorously on these and other problems as it had done on peace, the report adds: "Our survey does not suggest the way this should be done. It rather seems to reveal that we are not feeling forcibly enough that *anything* needs to be done."

Jane's manner of formulating the report showed her grasp of the needs of the Yearly Meeting as conclusively as did her originating and directing of the questionnaire. In the replies there had been a deep concern for the religious spirit in the meetings for worship, satisfaction with the basis of silent search, but desire for better vocal expression. To meet this need for improved preaching we find a suggestion straight from Jane's own hand.

> People accustomed to filling their minds continuously with the affairs of the material world cannot hope to worship satisfactorily by reason of entering a meeting house and taking a seat. Worship must be prepared for by meditation outside of the meeting hour, by reading inspirational literature, by study, and by habits of living and thinking as human beings doing their small part in a divine plan.

Nowhere was the penetration of Jane's mind more valuable to the Yearly Meeting than in the thought she gave to the care and expenditures of its funds. Already, before her appointment to the Representative Committee, several of the Jeanes gifts had come in. Besides the Samuel Jeanes Fund of $200,000 for educational purposes given by Anna T. Jeanes in 1895 and the Mary Jeanes Fund of $30,000 for student aid in 1900, which have been already described, Anna Jeanes had presented in 1896 the Joseph Jeanes Fund of $200,000 to establish and maintain boarding homes for the aged and infirm in the Quarterly Meetings, and in 1899 the Samuel Jeanes Fund of $100,000 to assist in the repair and construction of meeting houses. It was said that this last gift was prompted by a remark of her coachman as he drove her past a country meeting house. "It's too bad the Quakers always have such run-down looking churches," he said. The man's observation and his employer's resultant action have made a material change in the appearance of many of the buildings.

Jane recalls the origin of another of Anna Jeanes' gifts. One day this Friend saw workmen laying out the ground plans in preparation for the erection of the Young Friends Association building at 140 North Fifteenth Street (later enlarged as the Whittier Hotel). This involved tearing down some old houses. She stopped and asked why they were not going all the way to the corner of Cherry Street. They told her that someone else owned that lot. "I am the owner. I direct you to take down that building," she is reported to have said. Whether or not the story is factual, she did transfer that property to the Yearly Meeting, and the new structure included the corner site. Later the Representative Committee transferred the title of this portion of the land to the Young Friends Association.

As these impressive donations poured into the coffers of the Yearly Meeting, the Trustees felt that both they and the Meeting should be under greater legal protection, and they obtained in 1898 a charter of incorporation from the state. Alfred Moore was the first president of the legalized body.

This same careful lawyer was summoned by Anna Jeanes when she wished to make her will. As they talked over its possible provisions, her counsel offered a few suggestions. "I sent for thee to write my will, not to tell me what to put in it," she said tartly.

Anna Jeanes died in 1907. It was then learned that she still had important sums to dispose of. One of her largest bequests was of a million dollars to be used for the education of Negroes in the South. This fund, not under the care of Friends, is still an active factor in lifting the level of rural schools for Negroes throughout the South. She made gifts to hospitals, schools for the blind, children's homes, and other public benefits, and she increased her largess to the Yearly Meeting. She bequeathed $20,000 to the Philanthropic Committee for its work; she created a further fund under her brother Joseph's name of $250,000 to establish infirmaries in connection with the boarding homes; she set up a bequest amounting to $35,000 for the assistance of disabled women Friends in these homes; she devised the Stapeley Farm Fund of $100,000 for additional support of the homes and infirmaries; finally she left her residuary estate, originally about a million and a half dollars, to establish what is now known as the Jeanes Hospital.

While some of these funds were depleted by losses during the depression of the 1930's, others have been increased. There is a special Joseph Jeanes fund of invested income amounting to $16,000 which is used for the boarding-home infirmaries. The income of the residuary estate was added to the principal for some years before the hospital was built until now the endowment, including building and grounds, totals about three and a half millions. Although the Trustees hold and manage all the Jeanes Hospital funds by permission of the Yearly Meeting, the disposal is in the hands, not of a committee of the Yearly Meeting's selection, but of one appointed out of (or actually at present by) the Quarterly Meeting Home Committees—an odd quirk in Anna Jeanes' bequest.

The Trustees also care for, it might be added, a number of other funds besides those given by Anna T. Jeanes. The income of some of these goes directly to the Yearly Meeting. That accruing from more than $700,000 willed to George School is paid directly to the school's committee at the direction each year of the Yearly Meeting. Other income is specified by donors for philanthropic work, and is so allocated by the Finance Committee. In addition, with the consent of the Yearly Meeting or Representative Committee, the moneys handled by the Trustees include sums bequeathed for the benefit of certain subordinate Meetings, Friends' Central School, Friends Neighborhood Guild, and other activities, in none of which the Yearly Meeting has any financial interest.

UNDER WEIGHTY APPOINTMENT

During the period that the Yearly Meeting had very little money to spend, it was customary to make minutes granting permission to committees to draw on the treasurer for necessary expenses. Later the committees began to ask for fixed sums when their reports were made, and a Budget Committee was established on which representatives of the asking committees served. It was natural for each member to feel that the committee to which he belonged really needed money more than the others, so that it was difficult to have impartial judgment on the division. After the income from the Emma R. Comly Fund became available in 1935 and much more money was on hand for the extension of work, Jane Rushmore proposed that a new financial system be worked out and operated under a new Finance Committee. The idea was approved and turned over to the Representative Committee to implement.

Jane was at this time, of course, clerk of the Representative Committee and as such felt a great responsibility in regard to the money in its care and in its disposition. She had already persuaded it to provide more careful regulations for administering the income of the Samuel Jeanes Fund for meeting houses. She now gave her attention to the larger financial problem, developing its plan with the aid of an able lawyer and financier, Howard Cooper Johnson, who was just retiring from seventeen years' service on the Representative Committee. He was serving his sixteenth year as one of the Yearly Meeting Trustees and his third as president of that body. The recommended plan, adopted by the Yearly Meeting of 1936, provides careful advance study of the financial operations and needs of committees and affiliated interests by a small group within the Finance Committee. The same group also studies the amount that can reasonably be raised by local Meeting quotas. The Finance Committee then presents to the Representative Committee its recommendations for securing and distributing the funds. Approval by the Representative Committee is necessary before the budget is forwarded to the Yearly Meeting for adoption. Any outside groups, such as Pendle Hill or the Friends Fellowship Council, must, in the same way as Yearly Meeting committees, lay their appeal for Yearly Meeting help before the Finance Committee, which will recommend or revise their requests.

One of the specific problems which concerned Jane Rushmore was the difficulty of fulfilling promises of funds to committees when the treasurer had little money on hand and had to depend upon collections, or quotas, forwarded irregularly by local Meetings. With the accumulated Comly estate income it was possible to set aside a treasury reserve of considerable size. Charles F. Jenkins, who as a former treasurer of the Yearly Meeting had often been obliged to borrow money temporarily to meet committee allotments, experienced great surprise when he heard of the large treasury balance instead of the three or four thousand dollars he had usually carried. On the occasion of Jane's eightieth birthday he contributed a poem which contained these lines:

> She watches all the little things, how money goes and where,
> And not a dollar's budgeted unless the cash is there;
> The wonderment of financiers, economists and scholars,
> The Yearly Meeting's treasury holds fifty thousand dollars!
> If Mr. Morganthau would take our Jane to Washington,
> Presto! No bonds would be required, all deficits undone,
> If he would only try her plan, receive the nation's thanks,
> For ne'er a dollar would be pledged unless 'twas in the banks.

Since the present financial plan has been in operation, unpleasant differences of opinion about money have never appeared in the Yearly Meeting sessions; confidence in the judgment of the Finance and Representative Committees is general and Friends have learned that the Yearly Meeting does not make appropriations except on the recommendation of the Representative Committee. The value of such careful oversight is the more appreciated by Friends as they have seen the Yearly Meeting's annual outlay rise from approximately $10,000 a year when the Central Bureau opened in 1911 to more than $65,000 in 1952.

In 1935 the Yearly Meeting received its first allocation from the trust set up under the will of Emma R. Comly, for which the Girard Trust Company was named executor and trustee. She had the disposition of the estate of her father, Seth Comly, and drew her will in liberal terms. She suggested but did not direct how the money might be applied for religious, philanthropic, charitable, and educational purposes, including publications. The income of this trust accumulated and was added to the principal during the protracted adjudication of the estate. The last annual amount turned over to the Yearly Meeting (1952) was $23,500.

The freedom granted in the general terms of the will has been very valuable in increasing the activity of the Yearly Meeting. Among the property improvements to which the money has been applied were converting the Cherry Street Meeting House into its present form and remodeling part of the old elementary school building into offices for the Friends General Conference and the *Friends Intelligencer*. Besides the help which the fund provides for the work of many of the standing committees, it also gives a considerable and important subsidy every year to the *Friends Intelligencer,* although the paper is not owned or controlled by Philadelphia Yearly Meeting except through its membership in the Friends General Conference.

Rapport has been extremely close between the Representative Committee, the Finance Committee, and the Trustees. This was particularly the case during the years when Jane Rushmore was a member and then clerk of the first, and Howard Cooper Johnson a member and then president of the last. As Jane considered new business for the Representative Committee to undertake, Howard Johnson was invariably generous of time and advice. While he was still on the Committee, Jane depended on him to bring to a halt ill-advised waves of emotion that occasionally stirred the sessions.

During the depression years Howard Johnson carried a heavy burden of responsibility for the Yearly Meeting. He gave great thought and energy to pulling the Trustees out of difficulty then. He set up a plan for a reserve fund which would withhold 10 per cent of income to recoup losses, asking all beneficiaries if they would be willing to have this done. Eventually all agreed and the protective fund continues to exist. He was the first president who made a report to the Yearly Meeting which the general membership could understand. Consequently, the Meeting itself was the more ready to support the counsel and action of the Trustees, though it had always been grateful for the important, self-sacrificing service of these unsalaried members who carry responsibility for the care of (1952) nearly six million dollars.

Howard Cooper Johnson remained a trustee until 1951, but he retired as president in 1946, the year after Jane retired as clerk of the Representative Committee. These friends of twenty-five years' working-together held a little pleasant interchange on their respective withdrawals. The president of the Trustees was at the time financial vice-president of Strawbridge and Clothier, one of the largest department stores in Philadelphia and one of Quaker origin. He wrote to Jane in April of 1945:

In talking with associates in my own department here at the store this morning, I made an unqualified statement that there was the smartest business person I have ever met, and that if thee had had some experience in merchandising and had another thirty-five years of expectancy, thee would make the best department store executive I could find.

More formally he addressed her after her actual retirement as clerk.

I have myself witnessed the forward march of Philadelphia Quakerism under thy inspiring leadership, and there has been no other person in the Yearly Meeting who has done so much to inspire the best in others and to gently retard useless chatter about inconsequential matters. It is rare indeed for such wisdom to be accompanied by a sense of humor which has been responsible for winning many victories for a just cause.

Jane's letters to him are not available, but she freely acknowledges her reliance upon his business advice, financial judgment, and devoted attention to the Yearly Meeting's affairs.

Among many strong and able members of the Representative Committee there were two others with whom Jane had close personal friendship, John S. C. and Emily Bishop Harvey. Their interests centered in their religious society: they gave dedicated service to the Representative Committee, to their home Meeting, to the committees on temperance and peace, to Friends Neighborhood Guild, and to Pendle Hill. John Harvey was a valuable member of the executive board of the American Friends Service Committee, and was one of the early supporters of the idea of a Friends House in Philadelphia. Both of them were never-failing in their regular attendance at Yearly Meeting where they took active part. The central concerns of Friends were their own, and they talked them over freely with Jane.

Jane Rushmore retired as clerk of the Representative Committee following the Yearly Meeting of 1945, and as a member of the Committee in 1948. Her twenty-seven years of work with this important body were widely recognized both officially and by messages from friends. A special minute adopted in November 1945 records:

> . . . deep appreciation for her able services and her valued leadership. . . . During the years that Jane P. Rushmore has served as clerk there have been significant developments. . . . In each [she] displayed forward-looking co-operation combined with sound judgment. The members of this committee have been greatly favored in the service of our Friend Jane P. Rushmore as clerk during her long tenure of office.

The report of the Committee to the Yearly Meeting of 1946 states, "Under her guidance the committee became a well-organized, smoothly functioning body," and refers at the end to "the foresight and efficiency of one who has had the welfare of her Yearly Meeting and the Society of Friends uppermost in her mind for many years."

Of the many personal tributes, that of John H. Wood in 1948 embraces the sentiments expressed or implied by most of the others.

> . . . all of my few years of associating with the committee and Yearly Meeting affairs have had thee as the one strong reliable figure with ideas and judgments which invariably suited me exactly. Thy expressions just always seemed so clear and fair that they eliminated further discussion and endless debate which so often happens when there is no one of strong character and wide experience and accurate memory to express what becomes a final decision.
>
> We shall miss thee very much, but my chief regret is that those coming on the committee will not be able to experience and benefit by listening to thee on the matters of importance to the Yearly Meeting which arise constantly.
>
> The Society of Friends, the Yearly Meeting, every committee, and each one of us owe thee a great debt — one that may be repaid only in the satisfaction which thee must feel over the years of worthwhile work done. I do hope that thee may have a long enjoyment as an observer without being too disturbed with mistakes that the rest of us make.

CHAPTER XI

Crumbling Walls

In the eye of history a religious group may achieve distinction by its peculiarities or by its impact on events external to itself. Its importance in spiritual power, however, depends on whether or not its members live in a state of grace. The most tender and the most searching of the "Queries" which Friends have addressed to themselves for some three centuries begins, "Are love and unity maintained among you?" Herein Philadelphia Friends had conspicuously failed at the time of the Separation. But while anger and passion and disdain boiled for years on both sides, slowly the heat subsided and the probing of the Query into conscience was felt. Unfortunately the cooling lava left barriers both high and thick. Even when individuals here and there crossed over and made friends with persons of the "other branch," any official action was still far away. Because the Hicksites had been the ones actually to walk out of the famous session of the Yearly Meeting in 1827 and had opposed the Elders and the Meeting for Sufferings, they were regarded as secessionists of unsound tenets by those who remained in possession of Arch Street Meeting House. The latter, while outnumbered two to one as the local congregations soon divided all across the Yearly Meeting, believed firmly that the Ark of the Covenant reposed with them, especially since they were the section recognized by the London Yearly Meeting.

The Hicksites, however, refused to consider themselves as secessionists or heretics. They had withdrawn, they said, as "a quiet retreat from this scene of confusion."

They proclaimed no new theology in their *Discipline,* they emphasized what they believed to be the earliest principles of Friends, especially that "God alone is sovereign Lord of conscience," and they insisted that under His direct guidance they had liberty to propound doctrine.

For a time the divergence increased by reason of the strong evangelicalism of the Orthodox, and the growing Hicksite stress upon the Inner Light. In the Inner Light the Hicksites found a divine illumination of the conscience as it is directed toward God, a vision of His supreme greatness, of His unlimited love, and some apprehension of the meaning of life within His divine purposes. On this immediate experience of God, on the freedom of the individual to interpret for himself what God requires of him, and to decide what intellectual concepts for him most nearly embody the truth, Hicksite Friends have solidly maintained their ground.*

In the first decades this emphasis took the extreme form of belittling religious education and theology. Because the authority of the Inner Light was considered superior to the authority of Scripture, the Bible was not extensively read except for favorite passages and texts. Friends tended, as Jane Rushmore has expressed it, to stress their disbeliefs rather than their positive testimony that individual belief should not be imposed by authority but should follow the guidance of an earnest search for truth.

Later generations of Hicksites recognized some of the earlier mistakes. They saw the need of a more reasonable understanding of the Bible and they made probably the earliest Quaker attempts to promote religious education.

* For further discussion of Hicksite views, see Jane Rushmore's *Testimonies and Practice of the Society of Friends* (Philadelphia, 1945) and *The Quaker Way* (Philadelphia, 1951).

Their continued opposition to conformity in dogma has led them to an increase in liberality and tolerance of differences. If they have not been strongly united in beliefs, they have been closely bound in love of liberty. If they have refused to agree that the essence of religion lies in theological doctrine, they have undergone fewer shocks with the discoveries of science and the so-called higher criticism of the Bible than did many of the generation which first met the impact of these new intellectual advances. For the Hicksite Friends the adjustment may have been often difficult, but it seldom shattered the core of their faith.

In the last half-century, Hicksite and Orthodox conceptions have constantly increased the area of their common ground. This is due, in Jane Rushmore's observation, to the increasing study of the Bible, newer translations of it, and to a more intellectual view of the long sweep of Biblical history. On the one side individual interpretations of Scripture wander less far afield when there is more accurate knowledge; on the other, doctrinal regularity is less firmly upheld by what Jane calls proof-texts, that is, texts used to prove a point. Even the very sharp differences that have existed on the two sides in their views of the nature of Jesus and the meaning of his death are now growing into understanding.

The prevailing opinion of many Friends in both branches, as Jane sees them, has now come to be that there should not be an attempt to prescribe a theological belief which all are required to accept, but that all should be encouraged to seek for, and adhere to, what seems true to them in view of inner divine guidance and intellectual study. As we move toward reëstablishing union of the two branches, she says, it is important to hold to the early principle of freedom, for by that road comes progress. We should value the experience of others and use it as a test, but we can never substitute it for our own.

The approach toward each other of the two sides has been a matter of slow growth. The Separation had for many years a paralyzing effect on religious development. The Hicksites tended to live to themselves, shut within their walls. A long passage of years was necessary before they realized that their usefulness would be greater if they looked beyond their own borders. That idea was just beginning to emerge when Jane Rushmore became active in the Friends General Conference. She herself was one of the appreciable factors in inciting a willingness to change, in stirring to new vigor the quiescent and dwindling Society.

We have seen in former chapters that perhaps the very first steps toward a wider fellowship were induced by the visits of some of the English Friends, beginning with John William Graham's first trip to America in 1896. He was disappointed that his concern to bring the branches in America together did not bear fruit more quickly, but his work unquestionably marked an important start, for he on his repeated trips, and the other English Friends who soon followed, began an acquaintance highly congenial to Hicksite Friends, while the visitors, on reaching home, prodded London into recognition, in 1908, of the Hicksite group.

After 1900 some cracking of the walls had started between the two groups in Philadelphia, though scarcely noticeable at first. Leaders like Rufus Jones, Isaac Sharpless, and Charles Jenkins were determined to widen acquaintance and understanding. Small advances were made, though with much stumbling over hard rocks. There was, for instance, the occasion when Jane Rushmore wished to compare a passage in the Race Street *Discipline* with the equivalent paragraph in the Arch Street one, and asked a member of the latter Meeting if she might borrow her copy. "I'm sorry, but I don't think I could have my *Discipline* in the hands of a Race Street Friend," she was told.

In spite of rebuffs and difficulties here and there, friendship, mutual respect, and enjoyment developed at a slowly accelerating pace. The publication before 1900 of "News of Arch Street Friends" in the *Intelligencer* by Howard M. Jenkins, the friendly competition in sports which Charles F. Jenkins started soon after 1902 between the two Quaker resorts in the Poconos, the appearance of Cyrus W. Harvey, a Five Years Meeting Friend from Kansas, at the Winona Lake Conference in 1908, sporadic friendships arising between members of the two groups, were all good auguries. While in 1910 Robert Pyle of West Grove and Hannah Cadbury, an Orthodox Friend of Germantown, could not be married in the latter's own meeting house at Coulter Street but used the Hicksite building on School House Lane, only a few years later weddings between members of the two Yearly Meetings were accomplished in the houses of either side.

The Young Friends Movement, united from its inception in 1916, was heartily tramping down barriers in its bailiwick, determined that its generation would be free of old prejudice. Then came a purposeful effort to encourage mingling at the social level between older members of the two Philadelphia branches. In 1924 Henry S. Williams, an Arch Street Friend, with a small group including the indefatigable Charles F. Jenkins, initiated the Friends Social Union, composed solely of men on the theory that they were less well acquainted than the women. Approximately equal numbers from Race and Arch Street met regularly for dinner, an address, and a social evening. This became a popular institution, with wives later invited as guests. Charles Jenkins dubbed the adherents "Racers" and "Archers."

More influential than these social occasions, valuable as they were, was the rise of the American Friends Service Committee, formed in 1917 under the distinguished chairmanship of Rufus M. Jones. Its members forgot their differences in the importance of their common work. The group which organized the Committee was composed of Arch Street, Five Years Meeting, and General Conference members, the last of whom were Jesse H. Holmes, Lucy Biddle Lewis, Arabella Carter, William H. Cocks, and J. Barnard Walton. With no jurisdiction over any of the Yearly Meetings, this Committee now embraces representatives from nearly all of them throughout the country. Furthermore its efforts for reconciliation between hostile nations has made reconciliation ever more nearly a fact between the religious brothers in faith.

The development of the Service Committee must have hastened a concurrent movement toward union that perhaps was already on its way in the major committees of the two Philadelphia Yearly Meetings. By 1919 the two committees on peace were conferring regularly, and in 1933 they merged into a single body. The committees on race relations, temperance, and social order followed by becoming joint committees. The Committee on Education became joint in 1949, and that on Religious Education in 1952. The Business Problems Group and the Women's Problems Group, offshoots of the Social Order Committee and composed from the start of Friends from both

Meetings, have, as independent informal gatherings, conducted regular meetings for a number of years.

The American Friends Fellowship Council, established in 1935 with the direct aid of the American Friends Service Committee, is composed of members appointed by most of the Yearly Meetings in America, including Race Street. The Council has stimulated the growth of struggling independent Meetings and helped to start new ones which do not want to join any branch. These groups are urged to report to the Fellowship Council, which further encourages them to affiliate with a Yearly Meeting when they feel they can, for there is always danger that such independent units may wander from the main stream of Quaker thought if they are not in touch with any stable body. The Fellowship Council also maintains bonds with many individual non-Friends who are informally grouped into the "Wider Quaker Fellowship." The Fellowship Council has a constant close relationship with the Friends General Conference in service to these fringe groups.

Additional channels for coöperation among all American Quakers have been Pendle Hill, the school for religious and social study started in 1929, and the Friends Committee on National Legislation, formed in 1943 as an independent body to provide legislative information and advice on national government policies. Friends around the world have been brought into closer touch by the Friends World Committee for Consultation, established as a permanent outcome of the World Conference of Friends held at Swarthmore in 1937. In a great effort to draw all Friends together after World War I, London Yearly Meeting had initiated a World Conference in 1920; the second such gathering assembled seventeen years later on the Swarthmore College campus, with a number of delegates housed, and small group meetings held, at Haverford College, a few miles away. The occasion proved to be a further stimulus to all American Friends in awareness of their common ground. The World Committee which resulted from the Conference has worked ever since to fuse the small and scattered denomination into more unity of feeling and action.

Social mingling, work on joint committees, and participation in supraorganizations began to suggest united meetings for worship. Some twenty-five or more years ago a feeler was put out in that direction. A series of joint meetings for worship was proposed by Orthodox Friends to be held at Coulter Street, Germantown, for the members of that Meeting and the one held at School House Lane. The hosts somewhat anxiously made every preparation to have all go as smoothly as possible so that friction would be avoided and complete harmony prevail. In the course of the meeting a woman rising to preach used in her fervid discourse a highly evangelical turn of phrase. At the close of the session a much distressed Arch Street member approached Jane Rushmore. "I am very sorry about that Friend who was so excited over theology. I don't know who she is. We had hoped that nothing would happen to disturb any of you." "Don't worry," Jane replied. "We are used to her. She's one of ours." Perhaps the incident in itself helped both sides to see how artifical their barriers were.

A start toward organic union was made by members of these same two Meetings. In 1924 a few Coulter Street, School House Lane, and other members began to meet regularly together under the oversight of the two parent bodies. A few years later they built a meeting house in Chestnut Hill. When a change in the *Disciplines* of both

Yearly Meetings in 1933 made a new status possible, Chestnut Hill United Monthly Meeting was duly set up and acknowledged by the Quarterly Meetings of each branch, the pioneer united Meeting in Philadelphia. Its example was followed and the movement gained momentum. Besides new Meetings that wished to begin at once as undivided, many old ones have reached out to their neighboring Friends, now that their committee work and schools are united, and have found ways to combine Firstday schools, meetings for worship and for business, and, finally, properties. In 1952 out of a total of ninety Monthly Meetings in the two Philadelphia Yearly Meetings twenty-six are united, forty-two belong to Race Street, and twenty-two to Arch. Some Quarterly Meetings have become joint, but only one, Caln, is as yet completely united, an accomplishment of 1952.

Similar action is taking place between Hicksite and Orthodox Friends in other Yearly Meetings. Although the process varies with the differing situations, movements toward union are found in New York, Baltimore, Canada, Illinois, and other parts of the country. New England is already a united Yearly Meeting.

Arch Street Yearly Meeting has been the initiator in a number of friendly moves. Race Street was hesitant to act first, not wishing to push itself on the other Meeting, but has welcomed the proposals. In 1916 Arch Street first sent a copy of its general epistle to Race Street. In 1926 it was Arch Street that passed a minute authorizing certificates of removal to be exchanged with Race. This action, strongly advocated by J. Henry Bartlett, was a step of great significance, for it conceded a full recognition of Race Street members as *Friends*. In 1928 the Arch Street Yearly Meeting proposed an official visit to the sessions of Race Street Yearly Meeting.

On the day of this momentous overture the clerk of Race Street, Thomas A. Foulke, had to be absent and Jane Rushmore was acting clerk. Jane recounts:

> The visitors were formally introduced to our meeting and many expressions of satisfaction followed at this gesture of good feeling between the two Yearly Meetings. The following year Race Street returned the courtesy by sending five visitors to Arch Street. We were escorted to front seats in the gallery facing the meeting, and after a welcome to us we each seemed to be expected to say something fitting about the trend toward unity. After this interchange of visits all Friends were considered to be welcome attenders at the sessions of both Yearly Meetings.

Not all the overtures, however, were made by Arch Street. Charles F. Jenkins in 1931 printed and presented to both bodies a carefully thought out *Plan for Reuniting the Two Philadelphia Yearly Meetings of the Religious Society of Friends*. His proposal was to join the two groups at the top, let the Representative Committees iron out the difficulties, and encourage local Meetings to consolidate. The plan was received with interest, but it was premature because Friends were not generally well enough acquainted across the line and were not used to the idea of union. While it was not accepted, it challenged thinking and brought the possibility sharply before the attention of Friends. Now that the issue had been raised, it began to revolve in other minds. Meanwhile the fusions of subordinate meetings was increasing.

Then in 1945 both Yearly Meetings received a formal communication from "a joint committee of Friends for Montgomery and Bucks Counties" which forthrightly asked for the union of the two Yearly Meetings at once. The representative bodies were each directed to consider possible ways and means, and they appointed a joint subcommittee for the purpose. The Friends named to this undertaking met in a spirit of humility and search, though at the start some of them felt that their task was nearly hopeless. But when the will exists the way is apt to open. First, the Queries were made uniform for both Meetings and accepted in 1946. Then a plan was evolved, presented to and adopted by both Yearly Meetings of 1946, for an annual General Meeting to be held in the autumn to consider such matters and transact such business as the two Yearly Meetings might refer to it. The entire Race and Arch Street membership composes *de facto* the General Meeting.

November 1 to 3, 1946, saw the initial gathering of this new body. For the first two days it sat at Race Street, for the final day at Fourth and Arch. To most of those present, the occasion was one of deep thanksgiving. More and more Friends felt ashamed that the love and unity so precious to them as an outreach both to God and to their fellow men was violated in their own tiny segment of the Christian church. And to many the violation no longer had any meaning. Why should the artificial wall continue? These sentiments, however, were not yet general. History must still take its course slowly.

Discussion of the building up of spiritual reservoirs through the meetings for worship was first on the agenda of the General Meeting. Other topics were consideration of Quaker epistles from all over the world, reports from the American Friends Service Committee, the World Committee, the Fellowship Council, and the Committee on National Legislation. In succeeding years more and more of the joint committees of the two Yearly Meetings have asked to present their reports to the November gathering. The Yearly Meetings are still the grantors of authority to the General Meeting, which has no treasury and until 1952 no office or correspondent. Bills incurred have been divided between the two Meetings for payment and in 1952 the Central Bureau was designated as the address, with an assistant clerk as correspondent.

Side by side with the increasing efforts to attain a new fellowship between the Yearly Meetings came a wider problem of union among Christian churches. Two great interdenominational conferences were held in 1937 at Oxford and Edinburgh. To the latter of these Alfred C. Garrett was a delegate from Arch Street and at both Elbert Russell represented the Five Years Meeting. These conferences were the final steps preparatory to the formation of a World Council of Churches. To this Council all churches would be eligible upon their expressed agreement with one short statement: "The World Council of Churches is a fellowship of churches which accepts our Lord Jesus Christ as God and Saviour." Should Race Street Yearly Meeting be prepared to join on such a basis if, as seemed likely, it were invited?

The answer was not simple to find. A committee from the Representative Committee and from Ministry and Counsel studied the question. Their first report, circulated early in 1940, emphasized the fact that Friends have always been unwilling to formulate prescribed theological beliefs.

> It is not opinion, or speculation, or notions of what is true . . . or the subscription of articles of propositions, though never so soundly worked, that . . . makes a man a true believer or a true Christian; but it is conformity of mind and practice to the will of God . . . according to the dictates of this divine principle of light and life in the soul which denotes a person truly a child of God.*

So said William Penn, and so have said the Friends ever since. Strongly opposed as they had always been to any

---

* *Messenger*, Second month, 1940.

form of creed, most Race Street Friends also found the wording of the basic statement cast in a form not acceptable to them. However intense their allegiance to Jesus as Master and as interpreter of God through the Divine Spirit which transfigured him, they were not accustomed to referring to him as "God and Savior."

On the other hand as the report says:

> Christianity, neglected for years, is attacked as a degenerate vestige of an ancient past, and men are urged to concentrate their religious instincts upon a state, or a leader, or a race. . . . What chance has the Christian religion to bring salvation if its force is divided? . . . To unite Christendom as a world force for righteousness does not, as Friends see it, require a common creed or organic union. The essentials of unity are the love of God and the love of man, conceived and practiced in the spirit of Christ. But such love will not flourish in a vacuum of isolation. It requires contact. We must know our Christian brethren and share their labors. Indeed, Friends desire closer co-operation with Christians everywhere.*

Before Philadelphia Yearly Meeting convened, the Friends General Conference had received the invitation to join the World Conference and decision must be reached. Discussions at the annual session were serious and prolonged. At last Race Street Friends agreed that their members on the Central Committee should recommend to Friends General Conference a request that the World Council include the Conference "in any form of association which may seem right for a religious body which, never having required of its members the acceptance of any formula of belief, holds that the basis of fellowship is an inward experience, and that the essentials of unity are the love of God and the love of man conceived and practiced in the spirit of Christ." Similar minutes were adopted by the five other Yearly Meetings of

* *Ibid.*

the Conference, and the message was forwarded to the World Council. Bliss Forbush was appointed delegate from the Conference to the organizing meeting of the World Council in Amsterdam in the summer of 1948, the earliest that it could assemble after the war. After talking with many of the Council leaders, Bliss Forbush was convinced that Friends should be a part of this great movement.

The Yearly Meeting of 1949 was informed that Friends General Conference appeared to be accepted as a member of the World Council. Again misgivings were expressed as to whether such a position should be continued. Bliss Forbush came from Baltimore to explain at length that the Council did not regard their statement as a creed, that immense effort had gone into finding the simplest possible definition of all-embracing Christianity, that the churches had full freedom to interpret the words in their own way, and that if a denomination had any belief in the incarnation of God in man, any belief in God's power of salvation, then it was eligible and acceptable as a member of the Council.

His presentation won the day. In spite of reservations in the minds of some Friends, they agreed that this was no time to withhold from sharing the burden and concern of the whole Christian Church. They would greatly have preferred the wording of their own statement of essential unity. But the Council could not entertain the suggestion of a change, though it wanted Friends to join because of the practical work being done through the American Friends Service Committee. In the end all the Yearly Meetings in the General Conference agreed to its continuing a member of the World Council, at least for the present.

CRUMBLING WALLS

It is of interest to note that while London Yearly Meeting did not accept membership in the Council on the ground that the basis was actually creedal, Arch Street joined in spite of uneasiness at what they considered to be a definition of the undefinable. With their agreement to become a member they included this statement:

> In accepting membership in the World Council of Churches we wish it understood that we do not accept any doctrinal statement as a fixed dogma. No creedal statement can contain the truth regarding the significance of the Revelation of God in Jesus Christ — for that truth is a living truth, based not on words but on inner experience and it will inevitably be interpreted by different men in different times according to their ability and insight.*

Here was a different working out of Friends' belief in love and unity, and of their principle that interest in and helpfulness toward other groups were more important to the advance of Christianity than the wording of doctrinal statements. Friends had seen the devastating effect of noncoöperation in their own body. Unity in work and service seemed so essential that with the freedom of interpretation allowed to all, Hicksite as well as Orthodox were clear that they need not debar themselves from affiliation in furthering the Council's efforts.

When the two Philadelphia Meetings found themselves in agreement on this issue, there seemed to many members less reason than ever for postponing their own union. The General Meeting was a step forward in making common ground. But it was not what more and more Friends craved, the single and complete body of united Philadelphia Quakerism. It was at best a temporary expedient until the time should be ripe for actual amalgamation. Further impetus to the consummation was given on the

---
* Minute 52, *Proceedings of Philadelphia Yearly Meeting, Arch Street, 1949.*

return of Thomas and Eliza Foulke from Japan just before the Yearly Meeting of 1950. The Foulkes had spent a year under appointment by the American Friends Service Committee, Thomas Foulke as director of LARA (Licensed Agencies for Relief in Asia), and both of them as leaders of the new neighborhood center which the American Friends Service Committee was establishing in Tokyo. Both took active part in the Friends' Meeting there and became interested in all the Friends' activities. Both also became deeply aware of the tremendous misfortune of a divided Quakerism at home, which was hard to explain or condone on the other side of the world. They came back, on fire themselves, determined to kindle the Yearly Meetings of Philadelphia into forming some plan for immediate union. As a result each body appointed members to a joint committee to study how a complete union might be effected, and at the same time appointed another joint committee to compile a common *Book of Discipline.* These committees, at work at the present time, are making continual progress.

As Jane Rushmore watches the development toward union with keen interest, she remarks upon how generous the Arch Street Friends have been, how they have given up their isolation, proposed the study of united Meetings involving changes in both *Disciplines,* and time after time have joined the Race Street position. She feels that there is already a common basis of unity in the common Queries, the joint committees, the General Meeting, and the many united subordinate Meetings.

She suggests a clarification that may help to obviate some of the remaining difficulties. Faith and belief are closely related in our thinking, in Jane's estimation, but there is a distinction which we do well to keep in mind.

Faith is a spiritual quality. It refers to the direct relationship between God our Father and ourselves; it makes us aware of unseen realities. Belief is an intellectual quality. It may change for each of us as we develop more. We may all share the same faith, yet vary in our individual beliefs. It should not be hard to unite the branches on a basis of faith centering around our centuries-old profession of that Divine Immanence which we call the Inner Light, under whose guidance there can be freedom. But that freedom, Jane concludes, is not freedom to have no faith, nor freedom to act irresponsibly, but the accountable freedom to search for, *and then to follow,* the truth as we can discern it.

CHAPTER XII

The Active Eighties

On January 28, 1944, the day that Jane Rushmore was eighty years old, she was given a birthday party. At the luncheon in the auditorium of the Whittier more than two hundred of her friends crowded the long tables, bright on that mid-winter noon with quantities of yellow roses from her London Grove alumni. Hannah Clothier Hull, the gay and spirited toastmistress, called up speeches that were full of merriment, affection, and admiration for the guest of honor.

As expected, Rufus Jones opened his remarks with an appropriate story—of the Maine farmer who, on being asked, "Have you lived here all your life?" replied, "Not yit." Charles F. Jenkins brought his amusing "jingle," part of which has already been quoted in a previous chapter. After offering "full honors" to Jane's "three score years and ten," he went on:

> This was the phrase the Psalmist used, a ceiling date quite plain,
> Too bad he added that four score was sorrow, pride and pain.
> But old King David did not know, strumming his golden strings,
> Of vitamins and vaccines and new hygienic things.
> Remember, too, this time-worn truth, a dictum wise and weighty,
> Some folks are old at fifty-one and some are young at eighty!
> The Russians have their patriarch; the Romans Pius VIII;
> The Anglicans, archbishops created by the State;
> Thus every sect, in everyclime, has someone at the top —
> But now I see red lights ahead! Perhaps it's time to stop,
> And only add that there is one in Race Street Yearly Meeting
> Who night and day is on the job; we bring her loving greeting.

After a number of persons had recounted Jane's many services to Friends, Ruth and Irvin Poley appeared on the stage to give a skit of Jane interviewing Richmond Miller before he took his new job at the Bureau. This fairly brought down the house, so well were Jane's crisp sentences and imperturbable manner ever so slightly overdone.

Of the several happy poems produced for the day, an especially perceptive one was written by Richard R. Wood, an Arch Street Friend:

> Today we honor thee — thy spirit young,
> Thy ready wit, thy never yielding will.
> We bid thee, like Ulysses, onward voyage
> One equal temper of heroic heart
> To tell us that life's changing lights and shades,
> Its burden of experience, form an arch
> Through which the hitherto untraveled world
> Gleams brighter, broader-margined, with the years.
>
> 'Tis this in thee that gives encouragement —
> This dauntless, onward-pressing zest for life
> And those who live it. Fools are not by thee
> Gladly endured; and yet are we upraised,
> Not quenched, by thy quick judgments. In thy mind
> We feel potentiality of men
> To see the need, to do the deed, and rest
> In quiet, confident, untroubled faith,
> Serenely planning the next forward step.

The gathering at that birthday party was a fair demonstration of the scope of Jane's friendships. Her avid interest in people and her loyalty to her associates brought together pupils of half a century before, active businessmen who had served on committees with her, well-known Friends from Arch Street, her co-workers throughout Race Street Yearly Meeting, and her neighbors at home.

These neighbors have known a slightly different Jane from the woman of business capacity, direct thinking, and clear statement so much appreciated on working days. In the several places she has lived there has accumulated a

THE ACTIVE EIGHTIES

company of those who remember the candy-making parties, the nights she took care of their sick, the games she invented, the birds she could identify. When she and Emma Wallace settled on the edge of Riverton, N. J., they became unmistakably a part of the Quaker community there.

The house which they built in 1918 has almost always been shared by some other friend or relative. Dr. Mary Rushmore's adopted daughter, Alice T. Harwell, came there when she was twelve years old at the death of her foster mother. Her care and education to independent adulthood was a special responsibility, just as her appreciative disposition and constant helpfulness were a constant pleasure until on account of her health she had to live in the South. Blanche Early, a warm friend, lived with the family for several years, as did Anna Rushmore Irwin after the death of her husband. Recently Emma Wallace's widowed sister, Elsie W. Thomas, has been welcomed to the household.

A group of women, long-time intimates at Buck Hill and Riverton, has met for thirty years or more to read twentieth-century poetry. The extent of their explorations is attested by the variety of the books on Jane's shelves: Amy Lowell, Carl Sandburg, Katherine Mansfield, Louis Untermeyer, Edna St. Vincent Millay, John Masefield, Stephen Benét, T. S. Eliot.

To this home life Jane was, at the time of the birthday party, contemplating retirement. She had been gradually giving up some duties for several years, and, as we have seen, she did retire completely from her position at the Central Bureau the following year, when she was eighty-one. In answer to the frequent question whether it disturbs her to see others managing the office she ran for so long, she replies that she likes to go back to her former workroom "where the office force are my friends, and, according to an ancient legend, visiting them is like hyacinths for my soul."

The increased leisure of her later years gives Jane time to enjoy the simple pleasures of her home, the flowers that Emma Wallace tends, the birds that come to be fed, as well as the greater opportunities for social intercourse. Although she says she does not know how to pursue the last gracefully over the telephone, "I am learning," she adds, "to exasperate other persons on a party line by real visiting." And then she remarks, "In the cool of the evening I often walk in the garden and get the scent of the roses, most of them the gifts of Robert Pyle and his sisters. The fragrance of memories mingles with that of the roses."

She withdrew from the Finance Committee in 1946 and from the Representative Committee in 1948, retaining only membership on the Education Committee. To it in 1952 at the age of eighty-eight she accepted a new two-year term. The end of this period will mark seventy years of Jane Rushmore's service under Quaker appointment. Moreover, with most fields of her interest she is scarcely out of touch, for the now responsible leaders come, pilgrims to her door, to hear her clear judgment and progressive ideas.

Nor has she ceased being in demand to lead discussion and take speaking engagements, which keep her in touch with Friends in other Meetings. To no one was it surprising that in 1940 she was invited to give an important lecture under the William J. Cooper Foundation at Swarthmore College, and that afterwards a member of the faculty wrote to her, "I have talked with numerous

Jane P. Rushmore, Litt.D., 1952

members of your audience, including students, and find that all of them are enthusiastic about the job you did." Jane was only seventy-six then. Ten years later she led a discussion at Westtown with a group in their upper teens, that critical, unforgiving period. The following year the same group invited her to be one of their teachers, but she felt that she could not meet a night engagement. "I only wish," remarked Katharine H. Paton, secretary of the Religious Education Committee, "that I might have the wonderful experience of realizing that young people of high school age would desire to hear from me when I am eighty-seven years old." It was not an isolated occurrence. She had a similar reaction from a similar group the next year. A book compiled from Jane's writings, *The Quaker Way,* had been studied by a class at Merion Meeting led by Samuel J. Bunting, Jr. Then the whole thirteen boys and girls packed a supper and drove to Jane's house to spend a Sunday evening discussing the subject matter with her. "She is so alert," "So modern," "She told us funny stories," "She didn't give us the answer; said we ought to think it out for ourselves," "Oh, *yes,* we want to talk with her again," were some of the eager comments afterward.

For the 1951 Yearly Meeting Jane was asked to open the consideration of "Ministry" on the first afternoon, the most serious session of the whole week when the religious strength of the Society is discussed. After she had pleaded for more spiritual depth, more knowledge of the Bible, she closed saying, "We can rise to great heights only if we humbly ask God to help us, and then dedicate ourselves to helping Him." This day was a memorable introduction to the Yearly Meeting. One attender said that, after many of those present had shared thoughts which the address inspired, a feeling of benediction pervaded the company, and in the closing silence the united desire seemed to be, "Here am I, Lord. Use me."

Jane Rushmore's own spoken ministry is clear, thoughtful, and deeply religious. She enters upon no rhetorical flights, but stirs the conscience of listeners with modern applications of Biblical stories and truths. When families are struck down by grief, her ministry at funerals and her letters and messages have often been especially comforting and sustaining. Although she retains her membership in Philadelphia Monthly Meeting, the one next door to her home has so greatly benefited by her attendance that in 1945 a minute of gratitude was adopted for her "great contribution" to its "spiritual and intellectual life." As a suitable means of expression Jane was recorded as an honorary member of Westfield Monthly Meeting, the minute further stating "that there should be no financial or other obligation connected with the membership, and that it should constitute the Meeting's sincere expression of affectionate appreciation of thy presence among us." It is a gratification to Jane that Westfield is now a united Meeting. Many of its members of Orthodox origin were her good friends before the two congregations happily became one.

A pointed conciseness has always characterized her. A Friend sitting in Yearly Meeting overheard a whispered conversation behind her. "Who was the last speaker?" "Jane Rushmore. She says more in twenty-five words than other people do in twenty-five minutes."

It is not, actually, so much the compactness of her speech that rivets the attention of the audience as her ability to analyze and summarize the matter under consideration. She seldom takes part in the opening of a discussion. She listens as the various points are brought out. When all

THE ACTIVE EIGHTIES

sides have been pretty thoroughly presented, Jane's deep, strong voice, easily heard in every part of the house, speaks to the heart of the subject. As an active participant in many of the most important explorations of the Yearly Meeting she has often given a decisive word which crystallized the sense of the meeting. She does not intend or desire to form decisions. Rather, when the whole matter has been set forth, she sees quickly and acutely what others are groping for. She tries to be moderate in her statements, and a touch of humor usually disarms her critics. She does not mind being disagreed with, and respects a worthy antagonist. She does not press her opinion if the weight of the meeting is against her. But it seldom is, so great is the trust of many Friends in her judgment. "I wish that I could speak with the same terse directness that you habitually use. I wish also that I could feel my opinions were as sound as I always feel that yours are," said John W. Nason when he was president of Swarthmore College. Moreover, there is no forecasting how she will react to new proposals. She may disapprove a novel plan as unsound or encourage another as venturing into something new. "We need not be disturbed by experiments if they are made in good faith and sincerity," she said recently. And again, "Our fellowship is enriched by many types of experience and interpretation if they all represent a consecrated spirit and a humble reach for truth."*

All who know her well have been aware of her deep-running kindness, consideration, and understanding. She wants to help people, and in that simple statement lies much of her basic philosophy. Further, she gladly avows that if she has ever arrived anywhere, it is because of all the people who have helped her, beginning with the three

* *Messenger*, Fifth month, 1948.

big boys at Preston Hollow who made possible the winning of her first-grade teaching certificate. A fundamental respect for persons and for their sincere convictions is for her another feature of essential religion. "We must be tolerant of each other," she says, "not with a tolerance which does not care, but with the tolerance that cares so much that it would not weaken or destroy any belief that really helps individual members to live closer to God and reverently follow the precepts of Jesus."

Related to this respect for individuals is Jane's belief in the ability of ordinary people to achieve results. The lack of striking leadership in the Society of Friends does not distress her, who entirely ignores her own obvious place. She believes in the importance of the "little people." She once wrote in the *Messenger:*

> We have developed a very few great Quaker leaders. It is the faithful followers who with steadfast purpose have carried the torch which leaders had lighted, that are carrying the Friends' message to succeeding generations. Our progress is slow and sometimes halting because so often some of our members are content to be leaners rather than lifters. "Every great man is unique" but every common man is a unit potentially able to do his share of lifting. Cast your thoughts back over Christian history. How many really inspiring leaders can you name since New Testament days? Yet millions have done their bit to forward the principles taught by Jesus. If anyone who reads this little sheet is just a leaner, wont you try to see how much zest and interest it adds to life to step up and offer your strength as a lifter?*

Lifter Jane Rushmore has always been, but also something more. Through four decades she has been for the Society of Friends a steersman. Her clear eyes have looked into the future and helped to determine the course. Always for her the important thing has been the direction the

* *Messenger*, Eleventh month, 1948.

THE ACTIVE EIGHTIES

Quaker bark is taking, not who is at the helm. In her opinion neither as a pilot nor as a passenger does she deserve any special attention.

Nevertheless, she was selected for public recognition when in June 1952 Swarthmore College chose her as a recipient for an honorary degree. On a beautiful sunny morning she sat robed in cap and gown on the stage of the outdoor auditorium. For the last event of the program, which included the conferring of two other honorary degrees, she was called forward and presented by Joseph B. Shane, vice-president of the college. Then President Nason, addressing her and turning to the use of the "plain language" with unexpectedly moving effect, said:

> Jane Palen Rushmore, as teacher, minister, and writer, thee has devoted thy life to the service of God and of thy fellow men through the Society of Friends. Staunch in the defense of ancient Quaker principles, honest and courageous in recognizing the new demands of a changing world, old in wisdom and young in spirit, thy voice has been one of the guiding lights during this century of the Race Street Yearly Meeting. In grateful appreciation of thy many services to the Society, I confer upon thee . . . the degree of Doctor of Letters, and admit thee to all the rights and privileges pertaining to that degree.

The laurel of formal academic recognition, by her friends felt to be a happy and amply deserved encomium, sits lightly on Jane's brow. Her attention is upon the Society of Friends and its forward movement. She is still an influential Nestor in its progress. On the rare occasions when she does look back over its last two-thirds of a century, she might well appropriate the words of Aeneas: "These things I myself saw, and a great part of them I was."

Index

Abington Meeting, 117
Abraham, Emma, 98
Acton, Elizabeth, 12
Acton, Sarah, 12
Addams, Jane, 87
Advancement of Friends Principles, Committee on, 28, 75, 76, 79, 80, 83, 84, 97, 99, 104, 106
American Friends Fellowship Council, xv, 87, 105, 164, 170, 181, 185
American Friends Service Committee, xv, 52, 56, 82, 87, 115, 133, 134, 135, 163, 164, 173, 180, 181, 185, 188, 190
Appleton, William Hyde, 19
Arch Street Meeting House, 175
Arch Street Yearly Meeting, xiii, 80, 82, 94, 95, 118, 133, 136, 137, 148, 180, 183, 186, 189, 194
Asbury Park (N. J.) Conference, 91, 94
Ashworth, John, 95
Atkinson, James H., 107, 113

Baldwin, Bird T., 81
Baltimore Friends School, 67
Baltimore Yearly Meeting, 69, 71, 85, 87, 88, 89, 131, 147, 155, 183
Bancroft, Emma C., 81, 155
Bancroft, William P., 155
Bartlett, J. Henry, 147, 183
Barton, George A., 78, 94
Bartram, Anna W., 41, 44

Bartram, Frank M., 41, 107
Bartram, Mary S., 41
Bartram, Thomas Chalkley, 41
Battin, Benjamin F., 107, 108, 116
Beardsley, Arthur, 19
Benson, Robert, 54
Biddle, Clement M., 42
Biddle, Clement M. (Jr.), 121
Biddle, William C., 77, 99
Birdsall, William W., 72
Boarding Home Committees, 168
Bogardus, Joseph A., 27, 72
Bond, Elizabeth Powell, 27
Bonnell, Henry H., 64
Book of Discipline, see *Discipline, Book of*
Book of Meetings, 115, 162
Boston Society for Home Study, 23
Boughton, Alice, 64
Brinton, Anna Cox, 82
Brinton, Howard H., 82, 141
Brooklyn (N. Y.) First-day School, 28
Brooklyn (N. Y.) Friends School, 28
Brosius, Augustus, 75
Brumbaugh, Martin G., 65
Bryn Mawr College, 25, 94
Buck Hill Falls, xiv, 49–60, 78, 79, 195
Budget Committee, 138, 169
Bunting, Morgan, 50
Bunting, Samuel J., Jr., 197
Burdsall, Ellwood, 87
Business Problems Group, 180

203

INDEX

Cadbury, Hannah, 179
Cadbury, Dr. William W., 64
Calendar, The, 114, 162
Caln Quarterly Meeting, 183
Cambridge (Mass.) Monthly
  Meeting, 85
Camden (Del.) Meeting, 116
Camp Ill-Ind-O, 87
Camp Keewadin, 78
Canadian Friends' Service
  Committee, 86
Cape May (N. J.) Conferences,
  91, 99, 100
Carter, Arabella, 180
Central Committee, Friends General Conference, 74, 75, 97,
  98, 99, 106, 127, 187
Chambers, Frances Canby, 154
Chapman, Marianna, 25
Chappaqua (N. Y.) Conference,
  70
Chautauqua (N. Y.) Conferences,
  91, 94, 98
Cherry Street Meeting House,
  110, 111, 116, 118, 158, 171
Chestnut Hill United Monthly
  Meeting, 183
Civilian Public Service, 163
Clear Creek (Ill.) Meeting, 86
Clothier, Isaac H., 111
Coale, Edward, 72
Coale, Elizabeth, 80
Coale, S. Robinson, 50, 54
Cocks, William H., 180
Coles, William C., 107
Columbia Exposition, 70
Comly, Emma R., 131
Comly, Emma R., Fund, 169, 171
Comly, Seth, 171

Conferences, biennial, of Friends
  General Conference:
    Asbury Park, 91, 94
    Cape May, 91, 99, 100
    Chautauqua, 91, 94, 98
    Mountain Lake Park, 91, 95
    Ocean City, 91, 93, 100
    Ocean Grove, 91, 92
    Richmond, 91, 92, 99
    Saratoga Springs, 91, 99, 100
    Toronto, Canada, 91, 95
    Winona Lake, 91, 96, 179
Cooper, Lucy Smyth, 154
Cornell, Edward, 28, 77, 87
Cornell, Esther Haviland, 28
Cornell, John J., 11, 85
Coulter Street Meeting, 182
Courier, The, 122, 143, 146, 162
Cunningham, Susan J., 19

Discipline, Book of, 155, 156, 159,
  161, 176, 179, 182, 190
Discipline Committee, 138
Doane, Marcia, 104
Doane, Wilson M., 104
Dorsey, William M., 101–102
Drake, Israel, 1, 4, 5, 10, 11, 35
Drake, Jane Palen, 6, 7, 15
Drake, Mary, xvi, 16
Drake, Sarah Palen, *see*
  Rushmore, Sarah Drake

Early, Blanche, 195
Early Impressions, 102
Economic Problems, Committee
  on, Friends General Conference, 76
Education Committee, Friends
  General Conference, 74, 75,
  76, 106

INDEX

Education Committee, Philadelphia Yearly Meeting, 35, 42, 107, 111, 122, 139–142, 147, 155, 180, 196
Education Conference, 72
Edwards, Earle, 105
Elkinton, Anna Griscom, 118
Elwyn School, 18
Emergency Peace Committee, 133
Epistle Committee, New York Yearly Meeting, 26
Exercise Committee, 151
Extracts, 115

Fairfax (Va.) Quarterly Meeting, 89
Fellowship of Reconciliation, 82
Female Association of Philadelphia, 115
Fenn, William Wallace, 78–79
Ferris, Henry, 103
Finance Committee, 138, 168, 169, 170, 171, 172, 196
First-day School Bulletin, 77, 121, 128–132, 162
First-day School Committee, Friends General Conference, 74, 75, 76, 77, 83, 97, 106, 107, 112, 123
First-day School Committee, Philadelphia Yearly Meeting, 40, 107, 127, 131, 132, 148, 180, 197
First-day School Conference, 68, 69, 71, 88
First-day school lesson leaves, 127, 128
First-day School Union, 67
Five Years Meeting, 74, 81, 82, 94, 147, 180, 186
Flitcraft, Clement and Louella, 87

Flitcraft, Sarah B., 153
Florida Avenue (D.C.) Meeting, 89
Forbush, Bliss, 78, 88, 104, 188
Forbush, LaVerne, 88
Foulke, Eliza Ambler, 117, 190
Foulke, Thomas, 11
Foulke, Thomas A., 118, 184, 190
Founding a Home, 122, 162
Foxhowe Association, 51
Friends Almanac, 114
Friends Central Bureau, xiii, 66, 97, 106, 107–125, 127, 131, 136, 137, 148, 152, 162, 171, 186, 195
Friends' Central School, 48, 49, 65, 109, 110, 155, 168
Friends Charity Fuel Association, 115
Friends Committee on National Legislation, 76, 164, 181, 185
Friends Council on Education, 147
Friends Fellowship Council, *see* American Friends Fellowship Council
Friends General Conference, xiv, 28, 66, 68–106, 112, 114, 121, 122, 127, 131, 135, 147, 149, 153, 171, 178, 180, 181, 187, 188
Friends Here and There, 87
Friends Historical Association, 56
Friends Historical Library, 121
Friends Intelligencer, xv, 49, 56, 97, 101–103, 171, 179
Friends Intelligencer Associates, 103
Friends Neighborhood Guild, 168, 173
Friends Social Union, 179
Friends Year Book, 114

INDEX

Gardiner, Sunderland P., 26, 85
Garrett, Alfred C., 186
Garrigues, Matilda, 150
Gates, Thomas S., 62, 63
Gawthrop, Henry, 59
General Meeting, Philadelphia, xv, 123, 185, 189, 190
General Nominating Committee, 138, 154, 155, 160
Genesee Yearly Meeting, 26, 27, 71, 85, 86, 155
George, John M., 144
George School, xiv, 34, 42, 53, 54, 141, 144–146, 153, 168
George School Committee, 34, 53
Graham, John William, 72, 94, 95, 98, 178
Green, Samuel S., 19
Green Street First-day School, 67
Green Street Monthly Meeting, 56
Greenwich (N. J.) Meeting, 116
Gregg, Richard, 82
Griscom, Hannah, 7
Griscom, Dr. John, 101
Griscom, Samuel E., 49
Griscom, Sarah, 151, 152
Griscom, William Wade, 144
Griscom Hall, 58, 59

Haines, E. Vesta, 100
Hall, Lydia H., 102, 103, 121
Hallowell, Benjamin F., 45
Hallowell, Marguerite, 122
Hallowell, Morris L., 102
Hartwell, Rose, 16
Harvey, Cyrus W., 96, 97, 179
Harvey, Emily B. and John S. C., 173
Harwell, Alice T., 195
Haverford College, 47, 56, 80, 182

Hawkins, Harry A., 28
Haydock, Hannah W., 25
Hicks, Elias, 7, 8, 9, 28
Hicks, Philip M., 47
Higher Life, The, 122, 162
Hillborn, Rachel W., 102, 103
Hodgkin, Henry T., 82
Hodgkin, Dr. Thomas, 98
Hollingshead, Ellwood, 108
Holmes, Jesse H., 40, 79, 80, 83, 124, 134, 145, 180
Hoover, Herbert, 89
Hubben, William, 103
Hughes, John, 82
Hull, Hannah Clothier, 81, 135, 154, 193
Hull, William I., 81, 135
Hutchinson, John W., 27, 72
Hymnal, 77, 122

I Street (D. C.) Meeting, 89
Illinois Yearly Meeting, 68, 69, 70–71, 80, 84, 85, 86, 87, 96, 155, 183
Indiana Yearly Meeting, 71, 85, 86, 87, 155
Irving Street (D. C.) Meeting, 89
Irwin, Anna Rushmore, 13, 195
Irwin, George, 13

Jackson, Anna M., 27, 72
Jackson, Arthur C., 88, 104
Jackson, Caroline S., 152, 153
Jackson, John, 7
Jackson, Rachel, 7
Jackson, William M., 27, 71
Janney, Anna Canby, 154
Janney, Dr. O. Edward, 72, 81, 88, 92, 104
Janney, Robert M., 72
Janney, Susan W., 107, 111

INDEX

Jeanes, Anna T., 139–141, 166, 167, 168
Jeanes, Joseph, Fund, 166
Jeanes, Mary, Fund, 141, 166
Jeanes, Samuel, Fund for education, 140, 141, 160, 166
Jeanes, Samuel, Fund for meeting houses, 166, 169
Jeanes Hospital, 168
Jenkins, Beatrice, 87
Jenkins, Charles F., 49, 53, 55–57, 60, 103, 163, 170, 178, 179, 184, 193
Jenkins, Howard M., 49, 50, 57, 70, 103, 179
Jenkins, Marie C., 52, 163
Jenkins, Thomas A., 86–87
Johnson, Howard Cooper, 169, 172
Johnson, Jane, 102
Jones, Esther Holmes, 76
Jones, Mary Hobson, 137
Jones, Rufus M., 95, 178, 180, 193
Journal, The, 103

Kansas Yearly Meeting, 96
Kennett Monthly Meeting, 45
Knight, Rachel, 117

Laing School, 27
Lamb, Eli M., 67, 68, 88
Leidy, Dr. Joseph, 20
Lewis, Lucy Biddle, 135, 154, 180
Lincoln (Va.) Conference, 70
Lippincott, Mary, 82
Littleboy, Edith Winder, 86
Livezey, Mary R., 153
Lloyd, Elizabeth, 153
London Grove First-day School, 34
London Grove Friends School, 28, 31, 32, 139, 150
London Grove Meeting, 31, 34, 39, 41, 48
London Grove Young Friends Association, 39
London (Eng.) Yearly Meeting, 72, 94, 95, 98, 99, 175, 178, 189
Longstreth, Helen G., 102

Magill, Edward H., 19, 45, 70, 71, 72
Maris, George L., 145
Marot, Charles, 7, 20
Marot, Hannah Griscom, 20
Martin, Edward, 20
Martin, Samuel, 45
Martin Academy, 45, 46, 48
Matthews, Sarah W., 72
Meeting for Sufferings, 95, 96, 159
Mendelson, Dr. Walter, 62
Merion Meeting, 197
Messenger, The, 122, 162, 200
Miller, Richmond P., 122, 137, 162, 193
Mills, Albert T., 86
Mills, Clarence C., 86
Millville Meeting, 116
Ministry and Counsel, Committee on, 156, 161, 186
Mooney, Belle, 42
Moore, Alfred, 124, 154, 167
Moore, Esther T., 20
Moore, Frederick P., 20
Moore, George H., 20
Moore, Harriet J., 102
Moore, Joseph T., Jr., 20
Moore, Mary L., 20
Moore, R. Roland, 20
Moore, Thomas L., 20
Morgan, S. Rowland, 65
Morris, Anna Wharton, 136

207

INDEX

Mott, Lucretia, 22
Mott, James, 22
Mountain Lake Park (Md.) Conference, 91, 95
Murray, Augustus T., 89

Nason, John W., 199, 201
National Peace Conference, 76
New England Yearly Meeting, 85, 95, 183
New York Yearly Meeting, 10, 25, 27, 28, 71, 85, 87, 93, 96, 131, 147, 153, 155, 183
Norment, Caroline G., 82
Nutt, George H., 145

Oakford, Elsie, 100
Ocean City (N. J.) Conferences, 91, 93, 100
Ocean Grove (N. J.) Conference, 91, 92
Ohio Yearly Meeting, 69, 84
Orange Grove (Calif.) Monthly Meeting, 85, 116
Oswego School of Languages, 65
Overseers, Committee of, 161

Paiste, Henry T., 49
Pancoast, Charles E., 63
Parrish, Dillwyn, 11, 101
Parrish, Edward, 12, 101
Parrish, Isaac, 101
Parrish, Maxfield, 20
Parrish, Susan, 12
Parrish, Susanna M., 102
Paton, Katharine H., 197
Paxson, Alice Hall, 122
Peace Committee, Friends General Conference, 76
Peace Committee, Philadelphia Yearly Meeting, 134, 135

Pendle Hill, 78, 80, 82, 170, 173, 181
Penn, William, 186
Pennock, Charles J., 46
Pepler, Douglas, 95
Philadelphia Conference, 68
Philadelphia General Meeting, xv, 123, 185, 189, 190
Philadelphia Monthly Meeting, 118, 121, 123, 198
Philadelphia Quarterly Meeting, 121, 123
Philadelphia Yearly Meeting, Arch Street, xiii, 80, 82, 94, 95, 118, 133, 136, 137, 148, 180, 183, 186, 189, 194
Philadelphia Yearly Meeting, Race Street, xiii, xvi, 12, 29, 67, 70, 74, 85, 87, 96, 97, 105, 106, 108–125, 131–148, 150–158, 159–174, 181, 183–190, 194, 197, 198, 199, 201
Philanthropic Committee, Friends General Conference, 74, 75, 97, 106
Philanthropic Committee, Philadelphia Yearly Meeting, 107, 133–137, 148, 164, 165
Philanthropic Labor, Committee on, 69
Pickett, Clarence E. and Lilly P., 52
Pierce, Edwin, 96
Plan for Reuniting the Two Philadelphia Yearly Meetings, 184
Plummer, Jonathan W., 68, 69, 70, 72, 73, 86
Pocono Manor, 57
Poley, Irvin C. and Ruth V., 193
Potomac Quarterly Meeting, 89
Powell, Aaron M., 27, 72

INDEX

Preston Hollow (N. Y.) Public School, 24
Price, Ellen H. E., 107, 111
Purdy, Alexander C., 52
Pyle, Hannah Cadbury, 179
Pyle, Robert, 33, 37, 107, 108, 179, 196
Pyle, Robert L., 32, 35, 40, 53, 144

Quaker, The, 104
Quaker Way, The, 197

Race Relations, Committee on, 135, 136
Race Street Meeting House, 109–111, 158
Race Street Yearly Meeting, xiii, xvi, 12, 29, 67, 70, 74, 85, 87, 96, 97, 105, 106, 108–125, 131–148, 150–158, 159–174, 181, 183–190, 194, 197, 198, 199, 201
Randolph, Isabel F., 142
Religious Conference, 70, 73
Religious Education Bulletin, see First-day School Bulletin
Religious Education Committee, Friends General Conference, *see* First-day School Committee
Religious Education Committee, Philadelphia, *see* First-day School Committee, Philadelphia Yearly Meeting
Rensselaerville (N. Y.) Monthly Meeting, 4
Representative Committee, 98, 106, 111, 114, 122, 137, 154, 156, 159–174, 186, 196
Representative Meeting, Arch Street, 163

Richie, David S., 137–138
Richmond, Mary E., 62
Richmond (Ind.) Conferences, 73, 91, 92, 99
Roberts, Abby Mary Hall, 122
Roberts, Emmor, 140
Roberts, Isaac, 117
Roberts, Louisa J., 102
Roberts, Robert, 77
Roberts, Susan, 102
Robinson, Frances M., 86
Robinson, Louis N., 136
Rowntree, John Wilhelm, 94
Rushmore, Anna C., 2, 13, 195
Rushmore, Charles F., 2, 13, 15, 17
Rushmore, Edward Cary, 2, 13, 15, 16, 17
Rushmore, John Underhill, 1, 6, 7, 8, 9, 10, 15, 17, 18, 47
Rushmore, Mary D., 2, 13, 195
Rushmore, Sarah Drake, 1, 7, 8, 15, 47
Russell, Elbert, 81, 82, 186
Russell, Jane, 25

Salem (Ohio) Conference, 69
Sanford, Maria L., 18, 19
Saratoga Springs (N. Y.) Conference, 91, 99, 100
Scarlett, George B., 45
Scattered Seeds, 102, 121, 122
Schofield, Martha, 60
School House Lane Meeting, 182
Schuylkill Meeting, 116
Seaman, Robert, 99, 100
Shane, Joseph B., 201
Sharon Female Seminary, 7
Sharples, Alfred D., 144
Sharpless, Isaac, 178
Sharpless, William P., 102
Silcock, Harry T., 98

INDEX

Simkin, Robert L., 99
Smith, Esther Morton, 63
Social Order Committee, Friends General Conference, 76
Social Order Committee, Philadelphia Yearly Meeting, 137, 180
Social Service Committee, 137, 138
Speakman, Dr. William W., 49, 55
Spicer, R. Barclay, 103
Stabler, Charles M., 117
Stabler, Ida Palmer, 142
Stanton, Elizabeth Cady, 22
Stapeley Farm Fund, 168
Starr, Theodore, 61
Starr Center, 61–65, 105, 109, 127
Stern, Leon T., 136
Stirling, Anne Biddle, 135
Stover, Elizabeth, 28
Strawbridge and Clothier, 172
Streeter, Harrison, 154
Stubbs, Deborah F., xvi, 34, 36, 144, 145, 146
Stubbs, Dr. Joseph H., 34, 45, 145
Summer Schools, 78, 79, 80, 87, 95
Swarthmoor Hall, 98
Swarthmore College, 12, 17, 21, 23, 25, 27, 43, 47, 56, 70, 72, 87, 101, 121, 134, 135, 155, 181, 196, 199, 201
Swarthmore Conference, 72, 93
Swarthmore Friends Meeting, 23
Swayne, Amelia W., 131, 133
Swayne, David and Emmaline, 33

Teacher-training Class, 42
Teachers College, Columbia University, 46
Temperance Committee, 136

Testimonies and Practice of the Society of Friends, 128
Thomas, Elsie W., 195
Thomas, Howard, 47
Thomas, Dr. Joseph, 20
Thompson, Charles N., 53, 58
Thorne, Phoebe Anna, 25
Tilton, Josephine, 28
Tokyo (Japan) Meeting, 190
Toronto (Canada) Conference, 91, 95
Townsend, Anna A., 102
Townsend, Anne P., 141
Trustees of Philadelphia Yearly Meeting, 118, 154, 167, 168, 169, 172

Underhill, Charles F., 93
Union for Philanthropic Labor, 69, 73
University of Pennsylvania, 20, 21, 47, 50, 56, 62, 65

Wagner Institute, 65
Wallace, Emma Barnes, xv, 42, 44, 45, 47, 48, 49, 65, 100, 142, 195, 196
Walton, George A., 104, 146, 153
Walton, J. Barnard, 84, 105, 180
Walton, Joseph S., 36, 50, 58, 65, 79, 80, 145
Walton, Margaretta, 11, 28, 150, 151
Waynesville (Ohio) Conference, 69
Webster, Edmund, 140, 155
Westfield (N. J.) Monthly Meeting, 198
Wharton, Deborah Fisher, 12, 22, 28–29, 102
Wharton, Joseph, 50

INDEX

Wharton, Susan P., 50, 51, 59–65, 109
Whitman, Eleanor Wood, 146
Whitney, Charles A., 86
Whitson, Mary H., 107, 108
Whittier Hotel, 111, 166, 193
Wider Quaker Fellowship, 181
Wilbur, Henry W., 27, 74, 75, 79, 80, 83, 84, 99, 105, 107
Willets, Samuel, 87
Williams, Henry S., 179
Wilmington (Del.) Friends School, 42, 155
Wilson, Isaac, 27, 79, 85
Winder, Edith, 86
Winona Lake (Ind.) Conference, 91, 96, 179
Women's International League, 135
Women's Problems Group, 180
Wood, Herbert G., 95
Wood, John H., 174
Wood, Richard R., 134, 194
Woodbrooke School, 82
Woodbury (N. J.) Friends School, 7
Woodward, Dr. George, 63
Woolman School, 80, 81, 82, 83, 104
World Committee for Consultation, xv, 115, 181, 182, 185
World Conference of Friends, 181
World Council of Churches, 186–189
World Parliament of Religions, 70
Worth, Herbert P., 107, 109, 116
Wright, Phoebe C., 25

Yeatman, Lavinia, 28
Yellow Springs (Ohio) Meeting, 87
Yerkes, Sue C., 103
Young Friends Association, Philadelphia, 71, 109, 111, 166, 167
Young Friends Committee (London), 98
Young Friends Movement, xv, 117, 179

Zavitz, Charles, 86

DESIGNED by GUENTHER K. WEHRHAN
COMPOSITION AND PRINTING by ALLEN, LANE & SCOTT
BINDING by NATIONAL PUBLISHING COMPANY